The Abundant Kitchen

The Abundant Kitchen

A practical guide to making fermented foods, preserves & pickles

Niva & Yotam Kay

Pākaraka Permaculture

—

Photography by Aaron McLean

Skyhorse Publishing

L'chaim—to life—big, small, and microscopic.

Contents

Foreword

When we think about food, we often imagine a plate of delicious ingredients that ignite our taste receptors and satiate our hunger. Seldom do we stop to consider or appreciate the extraordinary journey these ingredients undergo before reaching our plates.

Welcome to the enchanting world of fermentation, where seemingly ordinary ingredients undergo a metamorphosis, transforming into extraordinary flavors, textures, and aromas.

Practiced and perfected by our ancestors for thousands of years and still cherished today by artisans, chefs, and hobbyists, fermentation creates new life from the raw, inert materials of the natural world through the interaction of thousands of communities of microorganisms, such as bacteria, yeasts, and molds. Some of these transformations may have come about by accident, but many are driven by sheer necessity with food being plentiful during one season then completely scarce the next. This profound transformation not only preserves food but unlocks hidden flavors, enhances nutritional value, and even unlocks health benefits.

The impact of fermentation on food produce is nothing short of remarkable. Consider the humble cabbage, transformed into tangy sauerkraut or spicy kimchi. With every jar of pickles, loaf of sourdough bread, or sip of kombucha, we partake in the fascinating history and legacy of fermentation.

But fermentation is not merely an exercise in taste and tradition—it is a powerhouse of nutritional benefits. As microorganisms work their magic, they unlock vital nutrients, increase bioavailability, and produce beneficial compounds that support gut health and bolster our immune systems.

Over the past decade the culinary industry has had a much-needed renaissance of this art and it has led to an exciting new wave and era of cooking and dish composition. With endlessly new possibilities, what at one point looked to be stagnant is now alive and flourishing.

Just like the cultures of beneficial microorganisms that are key to these transformative processes, Niva and Yotam have been adding huge value to their communities and everything they do in the food space. Inside these pages they have meticulously pieced together a guide that will confidently arm you with the ability to not only preserve the produce of your choice but also embark on a journey with them of this time-honored technique and uncover the profound impact it has on the realm of food production.

Their knowledge, understanding, and appreciation makes for not only a practical and educational read but also intertwines their own rich family history with this universal technique plus the love and joy that comes with practicing and passing such knowledge on to following generations.

I am fortunate to have been a recipient of Niva and Yotam's produce from their quarter-acre farm since the early years and have witnessed first-hand their passion and desire to create better food systems for not just themselves but everyone else they meet. There is a selflessness to their work that is akin to the transformative microbial work during a ferment, making me think it is by no chance they have applied said passion to these pages.

So, in an era where large food companies want food to have longer shelf life for the sake of profit, now is the time to harness this ancient form of preservation and celebrate the abundance and beauty of nature's seasons by honoring it in the truest form.

Food is life.

—Tom Hishon, chef and co-founder of Daily Bread, Orphan's Kitchen, kingi, WithWild

Introduction

When we were children, fermentation was the realm of our grandmothers. A refreshing dill cucumber ferment served with lunch on a hot summer day or a purple turnip pickle on a Saturday morning spread—the delicious homemade goods that you can only get when you come to visit grandma.

That changed quickly when we left home. Fermentation suddenly became an edgy and exciting magic that people would whisper about.

In our university dorms in 2006, a SCOBY (symbiotic culture of bacteria and yeast—see pages 94–97 for more) was handed to us by a fellow student with careful, and somewhat intimidating, instructions. Tales about the probiotic activity of sauerkraut were conjured and presented in class as if the cabbage had just been discovered. We were hooked. In 2007, we bought the first edition of *Wild Fermentation* by Sandor Ellix Katz. In addition to a trove of new flavors found among its pages, it gave us the confidence to safely experiment with every kind of fermentation in our tiny kitchen. For nearly two decades now, we have been fermenting, teaching, and sharing cultures; in all this time, we have never stopped learning and experimenting.

We now have our own trove of recipes, some that are staples in our home and others that are whipped up, in advance, for special occasions. We also learned to re-create those childhood flavors from the recipes handed down to us by our grandmothers. We are delighted to share them all in this book with you.

We wanted to offer recipes you can make with the stuff that grows in your garden. As much as possible, the recipes in this book use ingredients that we grow on our farm or otherwise source locally. One of the main privileges of a vegetable garden is to be able to use the highest-quality ingredients. This often means harvesting produce when it is at its peak and using it while it is fresh.

This book explores a wide range of practices to apply to that fresh produce, from lacto-fermenting, pickling, brewing kombucha, making mead and vinegar, baking sourdough, and meat-curing to koji mold-growing and complementary skills such as preserving and drying.

WELCOME

We experimented with each of these practices for many years, taking the time to learn their subtleties. While we have nearly two decades of experience in making and teaching these practices, and we present them in an approachable, easy-to-understand, and easy-to-replicate way, each of the chapters in this book contains only a fraction of what is possible—not everything we make would fit in. And we have much to keep learning about all of them, as well as expanding our repertoire to other fermentation and preservation methods that we have not yet had the chance to delve into. We humbly present these topics to you, knowing that each can, and often has, been expanded into whole books.

We are privileged to live at a time when peer-reviewed scientific research is readily available. Niva has spent numerous hours over many months fact-checking our work by reading scientific papers related to the recipes we included in this book. We discovered that the wild nature of fermentation means that there is difficulty in replicating experiments, leaving us with some unknowns or hard-to-conclude theories, questions, and findings. Nevertheless, we have experienced some humbling myth-busting in the process, and we have included some references in the footnotes that you can look up. We hope you enjoy the information delivered in this book as much as we enjoyed researching and presenting it to you.

We had a blast making all the recipes, again and again, this past year in our test kitchen to fine-tune for the book. We hope that following these recipes gives you the confidence to try new flavors and combinations and adapt and experiment with these techniques to make them your own.

Enjoy the journey and share your creations by hash-tagging #theabundantkitchen on your favorite social media platform.

Disclaimer

We share these recipes based on our experiences in our kitchen. We do not take responsibility for any health-related afflictions caused by attempting to reproduce the recipes in this book, and you will be making them at your own risk.

Glossary & Terminology

In this section, we want to establish a good understanding about certain technical terms we are using throughout the book. We all come from various backgrounds and we hope this will help clarify our approach for making foods and for you to better understand it, for great fermentation results.

Amino acids

Organic molecules that are the building blocks of all proteins.

Anaerobic process/conditions

Anaerobic digestion is a process in which bacteria break down organic matter in the absence of oxygen. In the kitchen, this is predominantly done by submergence in brine to avoid contact with air, or with the use of airlocks.

Backslopping

The act of incorporating an amount of a previous batch of a live-cultured food when making the next batch.

Bioactive compounds

Molecules found in small amounts in certain foods that have health benefits or therapeutic potential that is beyond their basic nutritional value.

Botulism

An illness caused by *Clostridium botulinum*, a toxic bacterium commonly found in the environment. The highest-risk foods are improperly canned and preserved low-acid vegetables and meats. Follow the advice in the canning section on pages 258–63 for prevention.

Canning

A method of preserving food in air-tight vacuum-sealed containers and heat-processing them sufficiently to enable the food to be stored at room temperature in the pantry. Canning is done by preparing foods, storing them in containers that are hermetically sealed (jars and bottles), and then sanitizing them using heat. For a detailed explanation of canning, see the preserves chapter (pages 258–63).

Cleaning

When making ferments and other live-cultured foods described in this book, it is important to pay attention to keeping things clean. By clean, unless stated otherwise, we mean:

- Food items should be clear of dirt.
- Working surfaces should be cleaned with warm water and soap.
- Equipment such as cutting boards, containers, bowls, jars, bottles, knives, and other utensils should be cleaned with warm water and soap, and rinsed thoroughly to remove any soap residues.
- Personal hygiene includes, but is not limited to, washing hands and wrists with warm water and soap; preparing food with clean clothes on; tying back your hair; and coming to the kitchen generally clean. Just like we all learned during the first stages of Covid, if you touch your face, your mouth, or your phone, wash your hands again.
- Any kitchen appliances you'll be using, such as a food processor or blender, should be thoroughly washed with warm water and soap.
- Use clean, filtered water for fermentation if your tap water is unfiltered or has a strong chlorine or fluoride taste.
- Keep your work area clean and free of clutter. Wipe down any spills or splashes to prevent mold or bacteria from growing.

Flavonoids

Naturally occurring polyphenolic compounds found in plants and in abundance in many fruits and vegetables. They are beneficial to health and play an important role in disease prevention.

Gluten

A set of proteins found in wheat, and similar proteins found in certain other grains (rye, barley) that have a viscoelastic behaviour. Gluten formation gives dough strength and stretchiness.

Gut microbiome

The trillions of bacteria, fungi, viruses, archaea, and parasites living in your guts. Unique to the individual, the gut microbiome is influenced by many factors, including diet, hygiene, and other environmental factors, and has an important role in many body functions, including digestion, mood, immunity, inflammatory responses, and more.

Headspace

Headspace refers to the air space above the food in a container and below the lid. This space is needed for expansion of foods as they are fermenting or processing. The extent of expansion is determined by the vigor of the fermentation process, the air content in the food, and the processing temperature. In fermentation and pickling it is best to leave as small a headspace as possible to reduce the chance of kahm yeast developing (see page 63). In miso-making we leave enough headspace to capture the tamari. In pasteurized foods, leaving headspace helps with forming a vacuum once the jars cool.

Hypha

One thread that makes the fungi mycelium (see overleaf).

Inoculation

The initial contact of microbes with a substrate. Or the introduction of the microbes to a substrate that they can grow on (for example, using backslopping to inoculate a new batch of the substrate with preferred microorganisms).

Lactose

A sugar found in milk and milk products. Around 70 percent of the world's population is lactose-intolerant and don't have lactase—the enzyme that hydrolyzes lactose into simple sugars in their small intestine after weaning.

Leaven

A combination of flour, water, and ripe starter, used to raise a dough. The leaven has a one-time use and is baked in the oven with the dough.

Litmus paper

A type of paper usually treated with natural dyes extracted from lichens that changes color when exposed to an acid or alkaline solution. It is a quick, reliable, and cheap indicator to test the acidity (pH) of drinks and foods.

Macronutrients

Nutrients essential to the body in large quantities, including fats, carbohydrates, proteins, and water.

Micronutrients

Nutrients essential to the body in small quantities, including vitamins and minerals.

Microorganism

An organism that can only be seen through a microscope. Microorganisms include bacteria, archaea, protozoa, algae, and fungi.

Mother

A general name for a starter or culture composed of bacteria and yeast, commonly used to refer to vinegar starter, kombucha SCOBY, and sourdough starter.

Mycelium

The body of fungi that usually consists of a mass of hyphae growing on a substrate or a host. Through the mycelium the fungi absorb nutrients.

Oxidation

A process in which exposure to oxygen chemically alters the substance.

Pasteurization

Pasteurizing is the process of heating food or drink to a temperature that is high enough to destroy the most heat-resistant pathogenic microorganisms and enzymes that can spoil the food or drink. Pasteurizing is used, for example, to remove any pre-existing microorganisms that might interfere with our chosen culture when making yogurt, in koji-based preparations to avoid mold contamination, and in canning.

Peptides

A molecule containing two or more amino acids similarly structured to proteins but smaller. Peptides include many hormones and antibiotics.

pH

A scale used to specify the acidity or alkalinity of a solution based on the hydrogen ion concentration. pH 7 is neutral; a lower pH number indicates acidity and a higher pH number indicates alkalinity.

Phytochemicals

Also known as phytonutrients. These are chemical compounds produced by plants, mainly to protect themselves from disease, infection, and consumption. Some phytochemicals are known for their medicinal and nutritional values; others for their toxicity.

Prebiotic

Compounds in foods (certain fruits, vegetables, and herbs) that are used by microorganisms (such as bacteria and fungi) in the host (such as humans), leading to a health benefit.

Probiotics

According to the World Health Organization, probiotics are "live microorganisms which, when administered in adequate amounts, confer a health benefit on the host."*

Room temperature

When discussing room temperature in relation to fermentation, it usually refers to the regular temperature in your home, which is typically within the comfortable range of 20–28°C (68–82°F). This range is optimal for many yeasts and bacteria, allowing them to efficiently transform our foods. It is handy to know your specific room temperature, as it can affect the fermentation process. For example, at higher room temperatures, such as 25–28°C (77–82°F), many recipes and processes will happen more quickly, while lower temperatures may slow down the fermentation process. Knowing your room temperature can help you set realistic expectations for fermentation times and adjust your fermentation process accordingly.

Sanitizing

Some foods are more sensitive to contamination than others and require sanitized equipment, such as all the recipes in the koji chapter (see pages 223–53). Sanitizing jars, lids, and equipment is also a good idea when making a large quantity of something or wanting to store something for longer with decreased chances of contamination.

---

* Colin Hill, et al., 'The International Scientific Association for Probiotics and Prebiotics Consensus Statement on the Scope and Appropriate Use of the Term Probiotic,' *Nature Reviews Gastroenterology & Hepatology* 11, no. 8 (August 2014): 506–14. https://doi.org/10.1038/nrgastro.2014.66.

Depending on how many jars you will be using, you might choose to use any of the following solutions. In all methods, it is best to sanitize each part of the equipment separately. For example, remove the rubber seals and lids from jars and sanitize them separately, and leave room between jars in the oven.

- Sanitizing can be done with high-percentage alcohol such as rubbing alcohol, and clean spirits such as vodka.
- Sanitize equipment by pouring boiling water over the clean items. Pour boiling water slowly over jars and bottles, a little bit at a time to avoid breaking glass from a too-rapid heat change. We use a bowl or flat tray to contain lids and cover them with boiling water. This is not a 100 percent foolproof method of sanitizing, but we find it works almost every time.
- Another option for sanitizing with boiling water is to place equipment inside a pot, cover it entirely with water and bring to a boil, then simmer on a low heat for 10 minutes. We very much recommend using either a rack that fits inside your pot, or specialized tongs that securely hold jars, specifically made for this purpose, to avoid hot water splashing and potential burns.
- A hot dishwasher cycle will do the trick.
- Place ovenproof items in the oven at 130°C (250°F) for 20 minutes.
- Sanitizing can also be done with a home-built or store-bought solar cooker. Many of our home-built solar cookers easily reach sanitizing temperatures. The trick here is that by using a relatively low heat, to compensate they will require more time in the solar cooker. Place the equipment in a solar cooker at a temperature of 65°C (150°F) for 1 hour.
- You can sanitize surfaces and equipment using food-grade sanitizers such as hydrogen peroxide, ANK anolyte, or DX50, which we use in our market garden's post-harvesting shed to maintain food safety, and they comply with both our food safety plan and our organic certification.

Caution: Glass doesn't respond well to rapid temperature change and can shatter or break. Heat or cool it gradually, and don't place cold foods/liquids in a hot jar or place hot foods/liquids in a cold jar.

We recommend always sanitizing one or two more jars than you think you need in case you need more containers. Aim for the sanitization to be completed close to when you will be ready to fill the containers. When using the oven, leave the door closed until you are going to use your equipment so that it doesn't cool down in the meantime.

SCOBY

A symbiotic culture of bacteria and yeast.

Sporulation

The formation of spores.

Starter

Also known as culture or mother, this is a preparation to assist the beginning of the fermentation process of various foods and drinks. In sourdough, the starter is a culture of bacteria and yeast that is maintained between baking.

Storage

When we refer to pantry storage, we mean an average temperature range of 10–18°C (50–65°F). This will allow food items to stay at a temperature that will reduce the growth of microorganisms and retain maximum nutrition.

When we refer to storing in the fridge, we mean a temperature range of 1–5°C (34–41°F).

Do not store foods at a temperature higher than 35°C (95°F).

Unless stated otherwise, place any fermented, jarred, or bottled recipe in this book away from direct sunlight in a cool part of your kitchen, with a relatively stable temperature range. Some recipes will call for placement in a warm location inside your house. Some of these warmer places can be close to a heater, in the hot water cupboard, or above the fridge (for us, it is also the solar battery/inverter unit). Always place active ferments on top of a tray, plate, or vessel that can capture any overflow and prevent a potential mess, as well as provide a clean surface for it to sit on.

Substrate

The base or medium on which an organism lives or grows and is supported by.

Tannin

Astringent phenolic substances that are common in plants. Tannins have antimicrobial properties that affect certain bacteria, including salmonella, *Escherichia coli* O157:H7, *Shigella*, *Staphylococcus*, and *Helicobacter pylori*.

Sourcing Ingredients

Sourcing ingredients for fermentation is another important aspect to consider. As with all recipes, the quality of the raw ingredients used has a massive effect on the end product.

Dry foods

When sourcing dry foods, purchasing in bulk quantities can significantly reduce the cost. This is one of the strategies we use to reduce our food bill and avoid excessive packaging.

Our recommendations for purchasing in bulk:

- Only buy items you use frequently and will likely use up in a reasonable timeframe, such as 3 to 12 months, to avoid food deteriorating.
- Check or enquire about the "Best Before" date to make sure it matches your consumption.
- Store bulk foods in an air-tight, insect- and rodent-proof container in the pantry or a location with similar conditions.
- Consider sharing purchases through a local food cooperative (or set one up).
- Reduce costs by buying straight from the grower, manufacturer, or importer.
- Purchasing large amounts of bulk foods, even at a discounted rate, can over-stretch your budget and storage capabilities. Start by purchasing small amounts of bulk foods and gradually build up your supply. Or start by sharing purchases with cooperatives, friends, family, and community.

Fresh produce

Generally speaking, vitamins are lost at a fast pace once vegetables and fruit are harvested, with more than half lost within a few days at room temperature, or in one to two weeks during refrigeration. Capturing produce while it is at its peak nutrition will increase the nutritional value of what you are making, as well as making it safer.

We encourage using locally sourced and organic produce as much as possible. Not only is it better for the environment, but it also ensures that the ingredients are of the highest quality and are not treated with chemicals or preservatives. Growing your own fruits and vegetables is a highly rewarding experience and results in the freshest possible produce. We often choose what to grow based on what we want to ferment and preserve. However, not everyone can grow the ingredients they need, and access to organic and local produce may be limited due to a lack of local offerings or financial constraints. When possible, we recommend looking for local growers, farmers' markets, and community-supported agriculture programs that may offer more affordable options for produce.

If buying from abroad, we encourage supporting fair-trade producers to ensure that the ingredients are ethically sourced and that the workers who grew them are treated fairly.

As gardeners, we learned to appreciate fermentation, pickling, and preserving as a fun and exciting way to diversify our diet, capture and preserve our seasonal bounty, and enhance the nutritional qualities of our homegrown produce. This includes those veggies that don't conform to buyers' expectations. It is a natural part of gardening that some veggies might be classified as "seconds" for their odd shape or because they seem less than perfect. However, when fresh they will not pose a food-safety issue, and will do great for many recipes in this book; we often use these "seconds" for bulk fermenting and preserving.

Vegetables and fresh foods have a high percentage of water, which makes them very perishable. Microorganisms such as bacteria, molds, and yeasts live and multiply quickly on the surface of fresh food and on the inside of bruised, insect-damaged, or diseased food. Enzymes in the food, the presence of oxygen, and uncontrolled moisture loss can all contribute to the deterioration of fresh food items.

To keep food at high nutritional value and safe to consume, pay attention to:

- using fresh ingredients
- carefully selecting and washing fresh food before use
- removing, trimming or peeling rotting or moldy parts
- adding acids (lemon juice or vinegar), when relevant
- using jars and self-sealing lids in good repair, which don't have any exposed metal or rust
- sanitizing jars correctly (see pages 21–22).

Collectively, these practices remove oxygen; destroy enzymes; prevent the growth of undesirable bacteria, yeasts, and molds; and help form a vacuum in jars. A good vacuum forms tight seals, which keep liquids in and air and microorganisms out of the jar.

Lacto-Fermentation

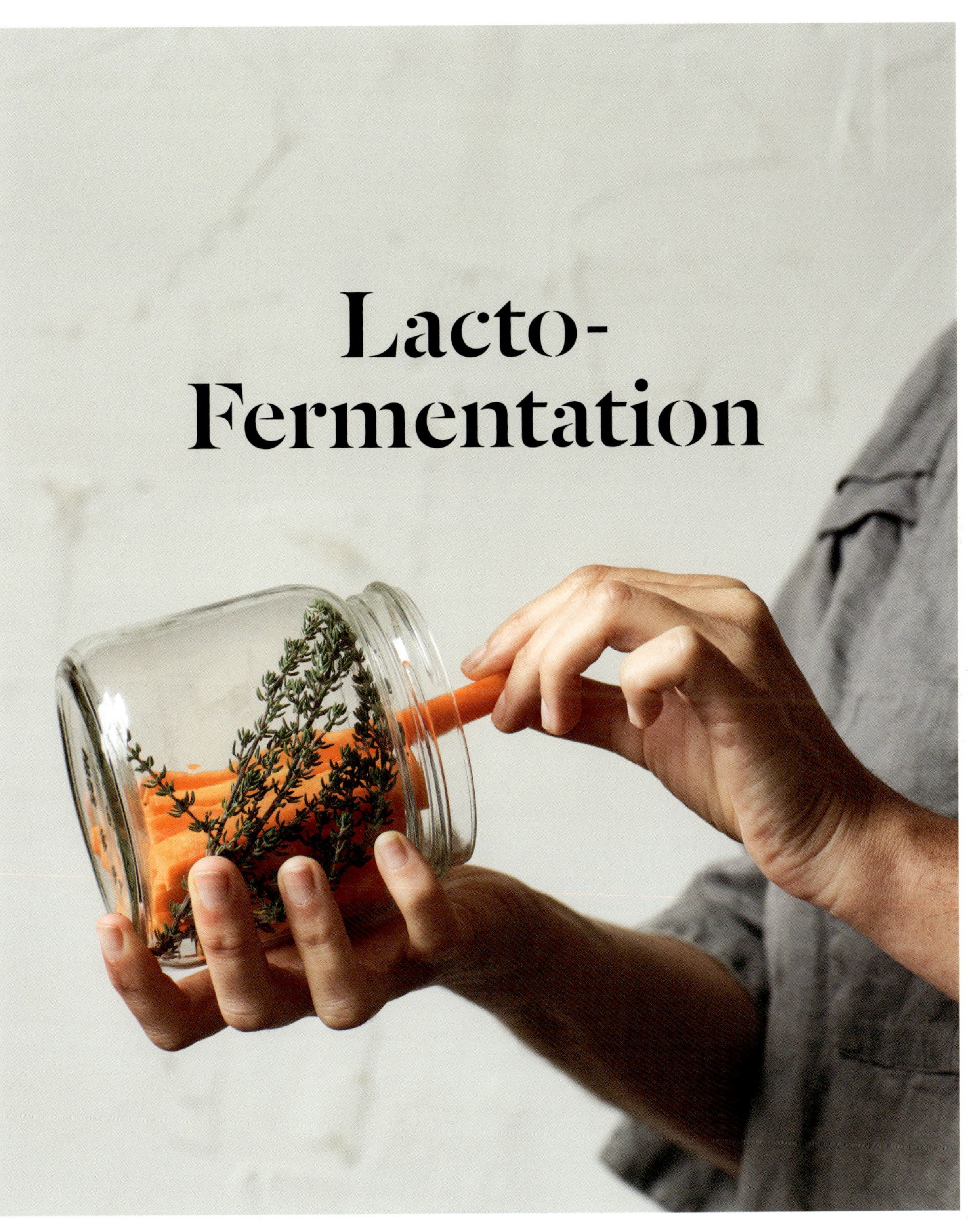

Lacto-fermentation is the type of fermentation done by a group of bacteria called lactic acid bacteria (LAB) and is one of the most common methods of fermentation practiced around the world.

LAB include a variety of bacteria genera that metabolize sugars to produce lactic acid. This acid environment created by LAB not only gives fermented foods their distinct mild sour flavor but also preserves and protects them from other microorganisms that would cause spoilage and decay. One of the benefits of lacto-fermentation is its accessibility, as LAB are found naturally all around us.

In this chapter, we have included recipes for lacto-fermented vegetables and dairy, as well as some recipes to enjoy them with. The potential to experiment and make combinations is practically endless—as long as you keep to the basic process, LAB will do their thing.

Lacto-fermented vegetables positively modulate the gut biome in ways that are beneficial to our digestive system and overall health and are potentially probiotic.[*] Like other fermented foods, they can make digestion easier, provide additional health-promoting nutrients not present in the raw ingredients,[†] and improve the intake of nutrients such as fiber, vitamins, and minerals.[‡] Lacto-fermentation of vegetables offers a good use for seconds—an "ugly" carrot cut into sticks or rounds is just as good as any other.

Lacto-fermented dairy, such as the well-researched and popular yogurt, is also high up there for nutritional value. Lacto-fermentation of dairy was shown to reduce lactose and galactose, and produce peptides, prebiotic compounds, and probiotics.[§] Lacto-fermentation produces amino acids supporting a safer gut environment, including by contributing to fighting pathogenic microorganisms.[¶]

LAB are generalists, and lacto-fermention can be done with a wide variety of ingredients. As long as LAB can access enough sugars and are supported by the right environment, they will convert sugar to lactic acid.

---

* Bryn C. Taylor, et al., "Consumption of Fermented Foods is Associated with Systematic Differences in the Gut Microbiome and Metabolome," *MSystems* 5, no. 2 (17 March 2020): e00901-19, https://doi.org/10.1128/mSystems.00901-19.

† Natasha K. Leeuwendaal, et al., "Fermented Foods, Health and the Gut Microbiome," *Nutrients* 14, no. 7 (6 April 2022): 1527, https://doi.org/10.3390/nu14071527.

‡ Vincenzo Castellone, et al., "Eating Fermented: Health Benefits of LAB-Fermented Foods," *Foods* 10, no. 11 (31 October 2021): 2639, https://doi.org/10.3390/foods10112639.

§ María García-Burgos, et al., "New Perspectives in Fermented Dairy Products and Their Health Relevance," *Journal of Functional Foods* 72 (September 2020): 104059, https://doi.org/10.1016/j.jff.2020.104059.

¶ Castellone, et al., "Eating Fermented."

Equipment: Containers, Lids & Weights

Equipment, surfaces, and hands must be thoroughly cleaned with warm water and soap every time you make, check on, and serve lacto-ferments. This level of cleanliness is suitable for many of the recipes in this book, but some recipes require additional precautions such as sanitizing and these will be discussed in the relevant sections.

Containers

Lacto-fermentation is an acid-producing anaerobic process, which requires the use of non-reactive materials, such as glass, ceramic, stainless steel, or food-grade plastic.

To make it easier to place ingredients, serve the ready-to-eat fermented food, and cover the surface area of the vessel with a weight, use vessels that are easy to access, such as wide-mouth jars. Using vessels with a low surface area to volume ratio is also preferable, to limit the exposure to air. It would come as no surprise then that our favorite fermentation containers are wide-mouthed jars, ceramic fermenting crocks, and, for larger quantities, food-grade buckets. Keep your ferments out of direct sunlight. A shady corner on your kitchen bench where you can easily monitor their progress, flavor, and health is the best.

Lids

There are several options for lids for your lacto-fermented foods. Whichever lid you go with, it is worth setting your ferments on a tray or plate to catch any overflow.

- *Slightly loose lids* — using standard jar lids and leaving them slightly loose will allow the safe release of carbon dioxide (CO_2) from the jar. If you use a tight clip jar, remove the rubber around the lid to loosen it and avoid creating a seal.
- *Airlock lid* — airlock lids allow CO_2 to be released safely while stopping contamination by insects and oxidation, which can result in surface yeast growth. Nowadays, it is easy to find simple silicon airlock lids and other fermentation-specific airlocks that fit in the ring of a preserving jar. Traditional ceramic fermenting crocks often include an outer rim for the lid to sit in that is filled with water and acts as an airlock.

  For more controlled fermentation, S-shaped airlocks, with the addition of a small amount of water in the lock, do a great job. We use them extensively in alcohol brewing.
- *Tight lids* — with lacto-fermentation and other carbonizing fermentation processes, there is a risk of CO_2 build-up in the jar, which can lead to an explosion.

If you use tight lids, you can "burp" your ferments occasionally by opening and closing the lid to release the pressure. Ensure the lids you use are in good condition, as exposed metal can react with the brine as it acidifies and can ruin your ferments. Tight lids are necessary for preserves and pickling. More on that in the coming chapters.

Weights

It is absolutely crucial that your vegetables remain fully submerged in the brine. Any bit that pops out and is exposed to air becomes a breeding ground for mold and other bacteria that will spoil the vegetables.

We love using smooth flat river rocks that fit neatly in the jar. Before the first use, we thoroughly clean and sanitize the rocks in boiling water. After the initial sanitizing of river rocks, it is enough to use warm water and soap for later use.

We also use ceramic weights, glass weights and, for larger quantities, inverted plates, and other repurposed items.

Basic Brine

Makes 250 ml (9 fl oz)

Brine is a solution of salt and water, and in many forms of fermentation and pickling it is the medium in which our ingredients are submerged. This basic brine is our most used brine. It has a ratio of 2 percent salt to water and is a great all-purpose solution.

Interestingly, salt is not strictly necessary for lacto-fermentation, which happens because of the activity of the lactic acid bacteria (LAB). These bacteria love anaerobic conditions and will show up to do their thing either way, with or without salt. As they do, the pH of the ferment will decrease, which will further protect it from harmful microorganisms.

But, since LAB are salt-tolerant, using a salt brine is an easy way to maintain their population while stopping harmful microorganisms from colonizing and contaminating our ferments. Salt has many other functions besides protecting the ferments. It is also used to draw out water from the vegetables to make up the brine in ferments such as sauerkraut, and to draw sugars from the vegetables to the brine, making it easier for LAB to feed on it. Finally, salt helps achieve crunchier ferments by hardening the pectin in the vegetables and reducing enzymic activity that promotes mushiness.

One to two teaspoons of salt per cup of water keeps our ferments safe and pleasantly salty. Use clean and unchlorinated water, or, if you are using chlorinated water, let it sit for a few hours before use. Look for non-iodized salt that doesn't contain additives or anticaking agents, as they can inhibit the beneficial bacteria from flourishing. We use natural New Zealand sea salt in our ferments. Sea salt is more mineral-rich than table salt, which also improves the overall crunchiness of our ferments.

If you can provide ideal and controlled conditions or are planning a very quick fermentation, no or low salt might be feasible for you. We highly recommend using this simple safety measure to create the best results, improve your chance of success, and minimize risks.

During the fermentation process, the brine soaks in all the different flavors in the jar, distributing them among all the vegetables in the jar. As a bonus, once you have finished eating, you can still use the brine for cooking, salad dressing, or as a straight-up tonic.

5 g (⅛ oz) salt
1 cup (250 ml/9 fl oz) water

Add the salt to the water and stir until the salt has dissolved.

3% Brine

Makes 250 ml (9 fl oz)

There are times when we will use a higher ratio of salt per cup of water, producing a 3 percent brine. When fermenting ingredients with a high water content of their own, such as cucumbers, we generally opt to increase the salt content to 3 percent.

In winter, when fermentation can take longer, and the pH drops more slowly due to the colder temperature, it can also be worth increasing the salt content to 3 percent. More salt will add a considerable safety margin, and will help keep your ferment from going too soft or spoiling.

7.5 g (⅙ oz) salt
1 cup (250 ml/9 fl oz) water

Add the salt to the water and stir until the salt has dissolved.

Tannin-rich leaves

A few examples of high-tannin additions, which help produce a crunchier ferment, include bay leaves, grapevine leaves, oak leaves (extra high in tannins, so use moderately), and raspberry leaves. Each has its own flavors to add to the mix, so factor that in when making your choice.

Our default, used in many of our ferments and pickles, are bay leaves and grapevine leaves, which we grow. Grapevine leaves are used in season from spring through summer. Our bay tree provides us with easy-to-access, year-round fresh and deliciously scented bay leaves.

Lacto-Fermented Vegetables

Whole Radishes in Brine

Recipe for 1 liter (35 fl oz) jar

We love making this ferment with breakfast or cherrybelle radishes and serving the radishes whole, as is, on each plate. Getting to know what a vegetable tastes like when fermented on its own—before trying it mixed up with other ingredients—is valuable culinary knowledge.

2–3 bunches of breakfast or cherrybelle radishes
(20–30 radishes depending on their size)
1 grapevine leaf
Basic Brine (see page 36), to cover

Rinse the radishes to ensure no soil or dirt particles are left on the skins. Grab each bunch about 3 cm (1¼ in) from the base of the radish and twist or cut the stems off so that each radish has approximately 2–3 cm (¾–1¼ in) of stem still intact.

Line one side of a clean jar with the grapevine leaf. Pack all the radishes tightly into the jar. Cover entirely with the Basic Brine and weigh down to keep the radishes submerged. Cover the jar with an airlock or a slightly loose lid and set it on a tray to catch any overflow. Keep the jar in sight in a cool location, and make sure to top up with fresh brine if the brine levels have dropped below the vegetable line.

Ready to start eating in 1–3 weeks. Keep in the fridge once you are happy with the level of acidity.

Salad Turnips & Fennel

Recipe for 1 liter (35 fl oz) jar

Salad turnips are naturally milder than radishes. In this recipe, they are complemented by fennel, which adds a nice aromatic flavor and goes with the turnips for a white veggie look. A couple of wedges of lemon are added to the jar to make a delicious zesty ferment.

Approx. 20 small to medium salad turnips
1 medium fennel bulb
¼ lemon
1 grapevine leaf
Basic Brine (see page 36), to cover

Rinse the turnips and fennel to ensure no soil or dirt particles are on the skins. Slice the fennel into 1–2 cm (½–¾ in) wide rings. Grab a bunch of turnips, and twist or cut the stems off so that each turnip has approximately 2–4 cm (¾–1½ in) of stem still intact. Salad turnip stems are great to eat, so don't hesitate to include them. Cut the turnips in half vertically. Check if the sliced fennel and turnip need another wash to remove any soil that was too hard to reach before cutting. Clean and slice the lemon into wedges, and remove the seeds. If there are blemishes on the skin, peel them off.

Line the side of a clean jar with a grapevine leaf. Mix the fennel, turnip, and lemon together and pack into the jar. Cover entirely with the Basic Brine and weigh down to keep the veggies submerged. Cover the jar with an airlock or slightly loose lid, and set it on a tray to catch any overflow. Keep the jar in sight in a cool location, and make sure to top up with fresh brine if the brine levels have dropped below the vegetable line.

Ready to start eating in 1–3 weeks. Keep in the fridge once you are happy with the level of acidity.

Herbed Carrot Sticks

Recipe for 500 ml (17 fl oz) jar

Easy to make and popular with kids, carrot sticks are a great way to introduce fermented food to any meal.

Approx. 15 small carrots
3–4 sprigs of thyme
Basic Brine (see page 36), to cover

Rinse the carrots to ensure no soil particles are left on the skins. If the skins are particularly rough or hard to clean, peel the carrots altogether. Cut the carrots into sticks and cut to the length needed to keep them below the brine line of your jar.

Line the jar wall with the sprigs of thyme. Hold your jar horizontally to make it easier to stack your carrot sticks. Add carrot sticks until the jar is packed tightly. Cover entirely with the Basic Brine and weigh down to keep the carrots submerged. Cover the jar with an airlock or slightly loose lid, and set it on a tray to catch any overflow. Keep the jar in sight in a cool location, and make sure to top up with fresh brine if the brine levels have dropped below the vegetable line.

Ready to start eating in 1–3 weeks. Keep in the fridge once you are happy with the level of acidity.

Dill Cucumbers

Recipe for 2 liter (70 fl oz) jar

In summer at Niva's grandmother Genya's house, you were guaranteed to find the tastiest, crunchiest homemade dill cucumbers (aka dill pickles). A permanent feature on the table, they accompanied every meal—breakfast, lunch, and dinner.

The key is getting the right cucumber. We grow Lebanese cucumbers, and when harvested young, thin, and firm, they are a perfect fit for this recipe.

12 Lebanese cucumbers
1 bunch dill
1 head garlic
1 chili pepper
2 bay leaves
3% Brine (see page 37), to cover

The first step is to soak the cucumbers in cold, even icy, water for an hour. This will make the cucumbers hardier and crunchier and help them keep their shape longer.

Once the cucumbers are cooled, start layering the ingredients in a clean jar—first some dill, a few garlic cloves, and then cucumbers. Compact vertically to form a crowded layer, then line the jar with more dill and garlic, and the chili and bay leaves and fit in as many more cucumbers as you can squeeze in. Weigh down and cover with enough 3% Brine to submerge the cucumbers and weight entirely. Cover the jar with an airlock or slightly loose lid, and set it on a tray to catch any overflow. Keep the jar in sight in a cool location, and make sure to top up with fresh brine if the brine overflows or drops.

Ready to start eating in 1–3 weeks. Keep in the fridge once you are happy with the level of acidity.

Dill Squash Sticks

Recipe for 2 liter (70 fl oz) jar

Dill pickle seasoning is perfectly delicious with other vegetables as well. Watermelon rinds are a classic example. When cucumbers are out of season and we have eaten up all our stock of dill pickles, we particularly enjoy this alternative dill pickle made with butternuts. It keeps the crunch factor high while carrying the lovely garlic and dill flavors.

The round part of the butternut, where the seeds are, doesn't work well with this recipe but is perfectly good to cook in any other way. Keep the skins on the butternut if clean, as they add a lot of crunch.

2 large butternut squash
1 bunch dill
1 head garlic
2 chili peppers
2 bay leaves
3% Brine (see page 37), to cover

Cut the long straight part of the butternuts into sticks and follow the method for Dill Cucumbers (see page 47), starting with the layering process.

Ready to eat within a week. Keep in the fridge, but don't wait too much longer to enjoy the whole jar as the butternut will soften into a mush. You can use the soft butternut by mixing them with the brine as dressing at that stage.

Utility

Beet Kvass

Recipe for 1 liter (35 fl oz) jar

By far the easiest fermented recipe there is, beet kvass is a simple drink that can be used on its own or in smoothies. It is an important ingredient in the hearty, sour beet soup borscht.

1 small to medium beet
1 liter (35 fl oz) water
5 g (⅛ oz) salt

Rinse the beet to ensure no soil or dirt particles are on the skin. Cut the beet into 2–3 cm (¾–1¼ in) cubes, skin and all. Place the cut beet in a clean jar and top it up with water. Stir in the salt. Cover the jar with an airlock or lid, and set it on a tray to catch any overflow. Sit it in a cool location, out of direct sunlight.

The beet kvass is ready from 1 week, when the liquid has turned a dark beet color. Keep in the fridge once you are happy with the level of acidity.

Berry Kvass Smoothie

Makes 1.5 liters (52 fl oz)

A great way to incorporate lacto-fermented beet kvass is to add it to a berry smoothie. Not only does it improve the nutritional value of the drink, but the deep beet color also naturally enhances the smoothie's color. You can use only a small amount for a mild, almost non-existent taste, or a more significant portion for a more adventurous fermented flavor.

2–3 bananas, peeled, chopped into chunks and frozen
1–1½ cups fresh or frozen berries
2 tablespoons (for mild flavor) to 150 ml (5 fl oz) (for strong flavor) Beet Kvass water
1–3 teaspoons sugar or honey (optional)

Place the frozen banana, berries and the desired amount of Beet Kvass into a blender.

Top up to the 1.5 liter (52 fl oz) mark with water. If the berries are fresh, use very cold water or some ice. Blend until the texture is smooth. Add sugar or honey if desired.

Serve cold in a clear cup so you can admire the color. You can store this drink in the fridge in a sealed jar for 2–3 days.

Sauerkraut

Recipe for 1 liter (35 fl oz) jar

Sauerkraut is undoubtedly phenomenal: just cabbage and salt transforms into a wonderfully tangy condiment that includes increased amounts of macronutrients, vitamin C, organic acids, and beneficial phytochemicals that are not usually bioavailable in cabbage.

In other recipes we've included variations of flavors, but in all honesty a simple sauerkraut is often all we want, nothing plain about it.

One medium fresh cabbage—by the time you have discarded all the outer leaves you should have approximately 800 g (1 lb 12 oz) of cabbage—makes 1 liter (35 fl oz) of sauerkraut.

We always make sauerkraut like Niva's grandma Genya did, by kneading it with our clean, bare hands. It gives the cabbage the best texture, and as our skin contains lactic acid bacteria, it actually helps the fermentation process.

1 medium cabbage
15 g (½ oz) salt
Spices, chopped veggies, or fruits of your choice (optional)
Basic Brine (see page 36), to top up if needed

Peel the older outer leaves off the cabbage and discard them. Pick one clean cabbage leaf from the new clean layer and set it aside to use later. Shred the rest of the cabbage. We shred our cabbages vertically with a sharp knife, rotating it to always be cutting the newly formed corners.

Place the shredded cabbage in a round bowl and sprinkle over the salt. Use the heel of your hand to knead the cabbage to draw the liquids out of it. Rotate the bowl as you knead to reach all the cabbage. As you knead it, the cabbage should make a crunchy sound. Keep going until the cabbage turns soft, the crunchy sounds stop, and liquids accumulate in the bowl. This liquid is our brine.

At this stage, you can mix in any spices—caraway and juniper berries are classic, but the possibilities are endless—as well as integrating other chopped vegetables or fruits.

(Continued on page 54)

Pack tight into a clean jar until the brine covers the cabbage. If not enough brine was drawn from the cabbage, top up with Basic Brine. Take the clean leaf that was set aside at the beginning and pack it on top of the kraut. This is known as a follower, and it is there to stop bits of cabbage from finding their way to the top and oxidizing. Weigh down to keep everything submerged under the brine. Cover the jar with an airlock or slightly loose lid, and set it on a tray to catch any overflow.

Keep the jar in sight in a cool location. Sauerkraut tends to be very active, and there is a good chance that brine will overflow and brine levels will drop, so make sure to top up with fresh brine as soon as possible. Sauerkraut is ready to eat when you like the level of sourness and texture. The longer you wait, the more sour it will become. Depending on the room temperature this can be within 1–4 weeks. As long as you keep everything submerged and use clean utensils to serve the jar, sauerkraut can stay out of the fridge; however, once the sauerkraut has reached the level of sourness you prefer, it is better to keep it in the fridge to slow further fermentation.

Amba Kraut

Recipe for 1 liter (35 fl oz) jar

This recipe makes a delicious yellow kraut, beautifully complemented with orange calendula petals (see photo overleaf).

In Iraq, amba is a spiced paste made with lacto-fermented green mangoes. As green mangoes aren't readily available to us here in Aotearoa, amba-flavored kraut makes for a neat alternative. Like the original, it is naturally soured, appropriately tangy and rich in flavor. Amba kraut is a delicious side dish to accompany all sorts of meat and fish, and the ultimate friend for Middle Eastern foods such as falafel, shawarma, and Sabich (see pages 58–9). It is also a perfect match with eggs in every style.

1 medium cabbage
15 g (½ oz) salt
1 medium white onion, sliced
Petals from 2–3 orange calendula flowers
80 ml (2½ fl oz) Homemade Amba Spice Mix (see page 57) (or if you are after a milder version, try 50 ml/1½ fl oz)
Basic Brine (see page 36), to top up if needed

Follow the Sauerkraut recipe (pages 52–3) up to the stage of mixing spices in. Add the onion, calendula petals, and spice mix into the bowl. Mix thoroughly.

Pack tight into a clean jar until the brine covers the cabbage. If not enough brine was drawn from the cabbage, top up with Basic Brine. Cover with a follower leaf, and weigh it down to keep everything submerged under the brine. Cover the jar with an airlock or slightly loose lid, and set it on a tray to catch any overflow.

Keep the jar in sight in a cool location and top up with Basic Brine as necessary during the fermentation period.

A key to enjoying this recipe is patience. This kraut needs time to sour to develop the rich and complex amba flavor. We recommend waiting at least 4 weeks before diving in!

Once the Amba Kraut has reached the level of sourness you prefer, you can keep it in the fridge to slow further fermentation.

Homemade Amba Spice Mix
and Amba Kraut (see page 55)

Homemade Amba Spice Mix

Makes 150 g (5½ oz)

This recipe is an alternative to store-bought amba powder, which is not usually available in Aotearoa. Commercial amba powder includes citric acid as a shortcut to the natural souring process. We have left it out. Like the original amba made with lacto-fermented green mango, in our fermented amba-flavored recipes such as Amba Kraut (see page 55), the acidity comes from the naturally created lactic acid. The amba in Amba Lemons (see page 288) receives its sourness from the lemons. If you are using the spice mix in non-fermented dishes, you might want to complement it with lemon juice or vinegar to achieve the sour edge that is so much a part of the amba flavor.

You can substitute the sweet paprika for smoked paprika for another layer of flavor; we find it works well. Double up the recipe as needed to make a bigger batch and use it for general cooking. In addition to being a fantastic addition to ferments and pickles, the unsoured spice mix is suited for cooking chicken, meat, and vegetable stews.

2 tablespoons mustard seeds
¼ cup fenugreek seeds
2 tablespoons ground turmeric
2 tablespoons sweet paprika

Place the mustard and fenugreek seeds in a spice grinder or mortar and pestle and grind them to a fine powder. Mix in the turmeric and paprika.

Store in an airtight jar.

Sabich

Serves 4

Originally a Shabbat morning meal for Iraqi Jews, this dish, stuffed in a fresh pita, has become a hugely popular Israeli street food. Amba sauce is a non-negotiable component of sabich, and luckily Amba Kraut fits right in to carry that weight.

Sabich is traditionally served with creamy braised eggs known as haminados—eggs that were cooked or roasted overnight in traditional "hamin" stew and soaked in its flavors, or roasted on top of Iraqi tbit (chicken with rice). Due to the long cooking time, the eggs change in both color and texture. We recommend using two- to three-week-old eggs, which are easier to peel than fresh-laid eggs.

This recipe uses large, black, teardrop-shaped eggplant, so if you use another variety, adjust the quantity accordingly. Choose shiny and light eggplants. When an eggplant is heavy with seeds, or when you see dull patches on its skin, it will be more bitter.

HAMINADOS (BRAISED EGGS)

4 eggs
Skin from 1 brown onion
5 g (⅛ oz) salt
1 tablespoon coffee or tea (optional)

FRIED EGGPLANT

2 shiny eggplants
Salt to sprinkle
Olive or sunflower oil for frying

TO ASSEMBLE

4 Sourdough Pitas (see pages 198–201)
¼–½ cup Amba Kraut (see page 55)
4 tablespoons diced tomato and cucumber (optional)
4 small potatoes, boiled until soft and sliced (optional)
Bunch of parsley, finely chopped
Tahini sauce (made from tahini, lemon juice, and water) (optional)

For the Haminados, bring the eggs to a boil in a saucepan of water, cover the pan with a lid to slow down water loss, then cook on low heat for a good few hours—the longer, the better. For best results, add the onion skin and salt to the cooking water. In winter, we often leave a pot of eggs on the woodstove overnight to get the desired effect. Don't be alarmed if the water content goes almost all the way down. Boiled eggs keep in the fridge for a week, so it is worth making extra for an easy feed later. It is common practice to add a tablespoon of coffee or black tea to the cooking water to enhance the color of the eggs, but it is not necessary flavor-wise. If you haven't planned this far ahead, a regular hard-boiled egg is entirely acceptable, and your sabich will still be filling and delicious.

For the Fried Eggplant, cut the eggplants into slices 5–7.5 mm (¼–⅜ in) thick. Set the slices in a colander and sprinkle with salt. Leave for 30–40 minutes, letting the bitter juice drip out of the eggplant. Wash the eggplant slices and pat dry. Heat the oil in a large heavy-based pan, such as a cast-iron pan. Fry the eggplant in a few batches, making sure to leave plenty of room for each slice, avoiding the slices touching each other. The eggplant drinks up the oil, so top up as necessary. Flip every 2–3 minutes, until the eggplant turns golden on both sides. Place on a paper towel to soak up the excess oil.

To assemble the Sabich, open the top of the Sourdough Pitas to access the inside. Peel the eggs. For each pita, place 1 egg cut into quarters or slices, a couple of big slices (or the equivalent in small slices) of eggplant, and 1–2 tablespoons Amba Kraut. Add any of the optional vegetables, if using. Sprinkle with parsley and drizzle with tahini sauce over the whole thing (optional but warmly recommended), or add the parsley to the tahini sauce.

Sauerkraut with Scallions, Radish, Chili & Ginger

Recipe for 1 liter (35 fl oz) jar

This recipe falls into the continuum that Sandor Ellix Katz, author of *Wild Fermentation*, calls krauchi. It is inspired by the rich flavors of Korean kimchi but is prepared with the sauerkraut method and flavor layering rather than the traditional kimchi method. We make this recipe when scallions are at peak season (in spring). It is a great way to integrate big amounts of it into the kraut and come out with a great tasting, nourishing krauchi.

300 g (10½ oz) daikon radish, sliced, and bigger slices halved
100 g (3½ oz) scallions, chopped
500 g (1 lb 2 oz) cabbage, chopped and kneaded as for Sauerkraut (see pages 52–54)
15 g (½ oz) fresh ginger, grated or thinly sliced
15 g (½ oz) cloves garlic, peeled and halved
3 cayenne chilies, tops trimmed
Basic Brine (see page 36), to top up if needed

Mix all the ingredients except the chilies and brine in a bowl.

Pack one-third of the ingredients into a jar as per the Sauerkraut method (see pages 52–54) then inlay one chili against the edge of the jar. Keep packing up to the top of the jar, laying the other chilies in as you go. Place a large slice of daikon on top of the other ingredients to prevent them from floating, and weigh down. If the accumulated brine is not sufficient to submerge the veggies, top up with Basic Brine. Cover the jar with an airlock or slightly loose lid, and set it on a tray to catch any overflow. Keep the jar in sight in a cool location, and make sure to top up with fresh brine if the brine overflows or drops.

Ready to start eating in 1–3 weeks. Keep in the fridge once you are happy with the level of acidity.

Krauchi

Recipe for 1 liter (35 fl oz) jar

Deeper still into the krauchi continuum (see page 60), this recipe uses a kimchi paste added to a regular cabbage that is processed in the sauerkraut fashion. We used to make kimchi in our workshops and on special occasions, but often we find ourselves processing a whole lot of cabbages for sauerkraut, then dividing and adding flavors for each jar. We started applying the kimchi paste to some of these batches and found that this allows us to enjoy delicious kimchi-kraut, in a way that works for us without having to plan for a separate process.

Miso is optional for the addition of umami and in place of traditional shrimp sauce.

KRAUT

1 medium cabbage, cut into strips 6 cm (2½ in) wide
15 g (½ oz) salt
10 scallions, green tops only, chopped (reserve the whites for another use)
350 g (12 oz) daikon radish (or other radishes), sliced into 4–5 mm (¼ in) rounds

PASTE

1 onion, chopped
1 thumb-sized piece fresh ginger (10 g/¼ oz), grated
40 g (1½ oz) dry Korean gochujang chili flakes or dried cayenne chilies, chopped (or as much as you prefer)
1 head garlic, chopped
2 tablespoons miso (optional)
Basic Brine (see page 36), to top up if needed

For the Kraut, place the cabbage and salt in a bowl and follow the instructions for making Sauerkraut (see pages 52–54). You want to leave a little bit more structure in Krauchi than in regular sauerkraut, so stop short of the point of not hearing the crunch sound. Add the scallion and radish to the cabbage and mix them together.

For the paste, combine the onion, ginger, chili and garlic and use a mortar and pestle or food processor. Stir in the miso, if using. The paste should end up evenly tinted red by the chili. Rub the paste all over the cabbage and vegetables. Pack into a clean jar and weigh down as you would with any sauerkraut. Cover the jar with an airlock or slightly loose lid, and set it on a tray to catch any overflow. Keep the jar in sight in a cool location.

Check the brine level after 24 hours. It should increase as the paste draws more liquids from the vegetables. If it hasn't, and your vegetables and weight are not submerged, top up with Basic Brine.

Ready to start eating within a few days to 2 weeks. Keep in the fridge once you are happy with the level of acidity.

Trouble-shooting for Fermented Vegetables

White film at the top of the ferment

One of the most common issues during fermentation is the development of oxidative yeasts. Known as kahm yeast, these can be a few different species of yeast that grow to form a white film on the surface of the ferment when sufficient oxygen is present. Kahm yeasts are not dangerous to consume, but they do pose a risk to the shelf life of your ferment.

Kahm yeast metabolizes lactic and acetic acid, which raises the brine's pH, making it susceptible to other organisms.[*] They also produce off-odors and flavors in the ferment.

If you see kahm yeast on the surface of your ferment, you can still eat it by skimming the film off carefully and discarding it. Transfer the ferment to the fridge as its acidity might be compromised. It is probably better to eat it sooner than later.

If kahm yeast is a frequent problem in your ferments and pickles, try leaving less air in your ferment headspace and opt for tight-fitting airlock lids instead of loose-band lids. Remember to always top up your ferments with fresh brine if the brine level has dropped below the weight.

Mold on the surface of the ferment

If your ferment smells rotten or grows mold in any color (not to be confused with kahm yeast), do not eat it. Mold cannot be skimmed off safely, as its filaments are invisible and grow into your ferment.

If mold grew on your ferment, sanitize anything that the mold was in contact with before using it again.

To reduce the risk of mold, make sure everything is clean—the jars, the cutting board, the knife, your hands, the weight, etc. And that vegetables are free of soil particles and are not contaminated with fungi. Use fresh spices to reduce the risk of contamination from the spices.

Make sure everything is submerged correctly. It only takes one tiny floating piece of vegetable to make a habitat for mold. You can also consider using an airlock lid instead of the other options.

Use the right amount of salt, or try adding a bit more salt. Use filtered water.

---

* M. J. R. Nout and F. M. Rombouts, 'Fermented and Acidified Plant Foods', In *The Microbiological Safety and Quality of Food*, edited by B. M. Lund, T. C. Baird-Parker and G. W. Gould. Gaithersburg, MD: Aspen Publishers, Inc., 2000.

Soft ferment

If your ferment is soft but otherwise smells and looks good, and your brine levels are fine, the most likely reason is that it has been fermenting in a too-warm environment. Try choosing a cooler spot or transferring your ferment to the fridge after 2–3 days to finish fermenting there.

If this is a recurring issue and temperature control has not helped, try increasing the percentage of salt in your brine.

When fermenting cucumbers, remember to remove the flower end, which contains enzymes that can soften the cucumbers.

Lacto-Fermented Dairy

Traditional Yogurt

Makes 4 liters (140 fl oz)

Making yogurt at home is rewarding on many levels and is relatively easy. When we make yogurt, we tend to make a large batch as it keeps so well in the fridge, and making more is hardly any extra work. When making yogurt, you have a lot of control over how to make it as you like it best: thick or thin and anything in between.

Any live yogurt can be used to make more live yogurt. We suggest inoculating your first batch using an unpasteurized yogurt you like, as you can keep many of its qualities. From then on, you can save a small amount in the fridge or freezer and use that as your next batch. Another option is to use a probiotic pill to introduce probiotic variants into your yogurt.

You should have everything you need to make yogurt already at home, and while a thermometer is handy, it is not a must.

We use a cooler to assist in keeping a large amount of jars at the right temperature range as the milk ferments, using hot-water bottles and other containers with hot water.

4 liters (140 fl oz) milk

60 ml (2 fl oz) fresh live-culture plain yogurt

Pour the milk into a heavy-based pot and heat over a low to medium heat, stirring the bottom frequently, until it bubbles. For thin yogurt, heat the milk to 60–70°C (140–150°F). For thicker yogurt, heat the milk to about 80–90°C (180–190°F), and keep it at this temperature for about 10 minutes.

Cool the milk to 40–42°C (104–108°F), or the point at which your (clean!) finger can stay in it without immediately needing to be removed. Pay attention and avoid letting your milk cool down to more than this point. We will often fill the sink with cold water and place the pot inside, which will help it cool down faster.

Mix the starter yogurt thoroughly into the milk so no yogurt pieces are visible. Pour the inoculated milk into clean jars.

Preheat the cooler by filling hot-water bottles with 4–6 liters (140–210 fl oz) close to boiling water, or use other containers, such as pots, bowls, and jars. If you find that the cooler doesn't hold the heat for 8–12 hours, replenish the containers with hot water midway.

Place the jars of yogurt in the cooler, with the hot water containers around them. Make sure to place any small jars, which don't have a lot of mass, so that they touch a hot container. After 8–12 hours, open one of the jars and check if the yogurt is ready. It should be pleasantly sour and a nice consistency. Store in the fridge for up to 4 weeks, and use within 5 days once opened.

Trouble-shooting for Yogurt

Milk hasn't turned into yogurt

If the milk hasn't turned into yogurt after 12 hours and is not sour, there could be two main issues. One is that the incubation temperature wasn't adequate, in which case replenish the hot water containers, leave them for longer, and maybe add a couple more. The second scenario is that the starter was added into the warm milk too soon and has cooked, or it was too weak to begin with, in which case you will need to re-inoculate the milk by reheating and following the recipe process again.

Notes for Yogurt

Using the correct jars

You can preheat the jars by rinsing them in warm water. Use jars in a size that will match your weekly consumption, as while the yogurt will keep well in sealed jars, it will not keep for more than a week once a jar has been opened. Remember to keep some in a smaller jar as the starter for the next batch. If you are making Labneh (see pages 71–72), use the largest jars you have, to reduce cleaning many smaller jars.

Storing yogurt for starting the next batch

Yogurt culture is alive and will degrade over time in the fridge and in the freezer. We find that when we set aside small jars, of 50–100 ml (1¾–3½ fl oz), to use as the next batch starter, they keep well in the back of the fridge (where temperatures are consistent) for up to two months, and make a great new batch. Storing your jar in the freezer should give you a window of 3 to 4 months before it is not suitable as a starter. When defrosting from the freezer, place the jar in the fridge to let it thaw gradually before using it. Fortunately, you can always buy a new container of yogurt and start again if your starter is no longer viable.

Dairy-Free Yogurt

Makes approx. 900 ml (32 fl oz)

Dairy-free yogurt is easy to make from raw nuts or seeds, or even easier using nut butters. When we were vegan, we made dairy-free yogurt from nuts and seeds frequently. It is very satisfying and sustainable to use nuts grown in your backyard or bought locally, and we suggest trying these options first before purchasing imported nuts.

To make dairy-free yogurt, you first need to make a relatively thick nut milk, followed by inoculation. There are several options to ferment the nut milk—we usually use a probiotic pill, but backslopping from a previous batch of dairy-free yogurt works just as well.

You can use pretty much any seeds or nuts you like to make the nut milk—hazelnuts, macadamias, walnuts, cashews, almonds, sesame, sunflower, coconut, soybeans, hemp, oats, rice, etc. They can be made into dairy-free yogurt individually or mixed in myriad combinations. Taste the nuts and seeds before using them to ensure they taste good and are not over-oxidized or too old.

Most nuts and seeds would benefit from soaking in water for 4 hours or overnight, making it easier to peel and blend them and resulting in a smoother, creamier texture. When using almonds, we suggest blanching them to make it easy to remove the skins.

1 cup nut butter or 375 ml (13 fl oz) nuts or seeds
1–2 cups water
Natural thickeners/emulsifiers such as tapioca starch, agar agar, xanthan gum, or guar gum (optional)
1 probiotic pill or 1½ tablespoons dairy-free yogurt starter
¼ teaspoon salt

If you're using nut butter, place the nut butter and 1 cup of water in a blender, and blend until thoroughly mixed. You want to get a smooth, creamy texture that is not too thick and not too runny. Slowly add more water until your preferred texture is achieved.

If you're using raw nuts or seeds, after soaking, drain, peel if necessary, and rinse the nuts/seeds. Add 1 cup of water and the rinsed nuts/seeds to a blender, and blend until thoroughly mixed—expect this to take 2–4 minutes. We find it easier to get a smoother texture when starting with a small amount of water, then add more water gradually until the desired texture is achieved.

Depending on the nut butter or nuts/seeds you are using, the strength of your blender and the texture you want your final yogurt to have, you might choose to strain the liquid through a cheesecloth or nut milk bag into a bowl, and make the yogurt from that. If your blended nuts are very smooth, in a texture you can see yourself enjoying them as is, you can inoculate them without straining. To get a nice creamy yogurt, you can thicken the strained nut milk with natural thickeners/emulsifiers.

Open a probiotic pill and empty it into the blender or bowl. Instead of a probiotic pill, you can use dairy-free yogurt or even regular yogurt (if you don't mind). Blend on low speed for a few seconds. Pour into a jar.

On warm summer days, you can ferment the inoculated dairy-free milk simply by leaving it on the counter or in a warm spot in the house for 24–48 hours.

On colder days, or if you prefer, you can ferment the inoculated dairy-free milk at a temperature range of 35–42°C (95–108°F) within 6–12 hours. You can use one of the following methods to heat the jar and keep it at the desired temperature: in a cooler with hot water containers, in the oven at 40°C (104°F), in a bowl with water at about 50°C (122°F), heat up to temperature and keep in a thermos or yogurt maker, or in a suitable dehydrator or slow cooker.

After 6 hours, you can start tasting it for readiness. If it isn't ready, let it sit for longer. If a liquid forms at the top, you can tip it out for a creamier texture. You can use this fermented liquid in smoothies.

Place in the fridge and use within 5 days.

Rose Honey Yogurt

Makes 1 cup

A perfect match of homemade yogurt and rose honey for a lazy summer morning (see photo on page 285).

2 tablespoons Rose Honey (see page 284), plus extra to drizzle
1 cup cold yogurt
Seeds from 1 cardamom pod (optional)
Walnuts, pecans, or pistachio pieces to top

Mix the honey into the yogurt. Grind and stir through the cardamom seeds, if using. Pour the yogurt into a tall cup, top with nuts, and drizzle more honey on top before serving.

Labneh (Strained Yogurt Cheese)

Makes 750 ml (26 fl oz)

Labneh is a hugely popular food across the Middle East, where before accessible refrigeration, making it was a common way to preserve the abundance of milk in the spring and keep it edible. Labneh is a delicious cheese made by straining yogurt and letting the whey separate. It has a mild sour flavor, similar to yogurt, but with a firmer texture that makes it suitable to use as a spread, similar to cream cheese. When it's condensed further it can be stored in balls under olive oil.

Use labneh as a dip (we love dipping veggies in it), or a spread. It is best served with a drizzle of olive oil and a sprinkle of salt, sumac, za'atar, or dukkah. If you don't plan to store your labneh for a long period of time, you can also make a herby labneh by mixing in herbs and spice blends, such as finely chopped garlic, chili, chives, scallions, parsley, mint, dill, basil, thyme, and oregano.

Labneh is an awesome breakfast food.

2 liters (70 fl oz) yogurt
2.5 g (1/16 oz) salt

Line a colander with cheesecloth or a lint-free kitchen towel, preferably with enough of an overhang to be folded on top once it is filled with the yogurt. Place the colander in a pot or a bowl that will allow the whey to drain off without touching the bottom of the colander.

Gently pour the yogurt into the lined colander and mix in the salt. The whey will slowly separate and drain, firming up the labneh as the hours pass. To assist the whey in separating, add a weight on top of the folded cheesecloth or towel or squeeze the labneh now and again. We often take a small plate and place something heavy on top of it—just ensure it is secure enough and won't tip off when the labneh level changes. Another option to drain your labneh is to tie the cloth with the yogurt and hang it somewhere out of the way (the shower is a pretty good option). We suggest the minimum time to let the whey drain should be 4 hours at room temperature. We prefer to give our labneh 8–12 hours, resulting in a denser spread which is *sooo* good.

(Continued overleaf)

You can go longer, even up to 48 hours, to get to your preferred consistency.

If you find the labneh too acidic for your palate, the next time you make it you can place the bowl in the fridge to drain and separate, slowing down fermentation while letting it drain.

Once the labneh is ready, remove it from the cloth. It can be now served or stored.

This creamy and lovely labneh requires refrigeration and will keep for a couple of weeks. Top it with olive oil to seal it for a slightly longer shelf life.

For longer storage, keep concentrating your labneh by letting the whey drain for 48 to 72 hours to achieve a firm consistency. Start by filling a wide-mouthed jar about one-third of the way with olive oil. Lightly oil your hands with olive oil and shape the labneh into balls 2–3 cm (¾–1¼ in) in diameter. Gently drop them into the jar, and top it up with more oil if needed to make sure the balls are completely submerged. This concentrated labneh, unopened, has a projected shelf life of up to 2 years.* When preserving labneh this way, avoid flavoring the balls, which introduces microorganisms that can spoil the labneh faster.

* T Keceli, Rk Robinson and Mh Gordon, "The Role of Olive Oil in the Preservation of Yogurt Cheese (Labneh Anbaris)," *International Journal of Dairy Technology* 52, no. 2 (1 May 1999): 68–72.

Pickles

Pickling offers a quick and reliable way to preserve vegetables and is one of the best and most common ways to capture seasonal bounty. We love how much the vegetables retain their form, color, and crunchiness, and the pickling process provides an awesome opportunity to add spices and herbs to make delicious blends of complementary ingredients.

Beyond preservation, using natural vinegar, such as homemade vinegar or unpasteurized apple cider vinegar, can remarkably improve the flavor of pickles. In our kitchen we primarily use our homemade vinegar (see pages 153–56). Some of our staple vinegars include apple vinegar, pear vinegar, apple and pear vinegar (we live on the edge), peach vinegar, kombucha vinegar, plum vinegar, and mead vinegar. White vinegar, made from distilled grains, is not our go-to, but if that is your preference, it will be perfectly suitable for making pickles.

When adding vinegar to a salt brine to pour over vegetables, the acetic acid in the vinegar immediately increases the acidity of the solution to create pickles. The increased acidity acts as a natural preservative. It vastly reduces the type of microorganisms that can live in the solution we submerge our ingredients in. It is food safety 101—low pH is inhospitable to harmful microorganisms.

All vegetables can be pickled, and pickling is a great way to preserve the abundance in your garden while transforming it into delicious foods. You can pickle individual vegetables or mix them so they are pickled together in the jar. While we mostly make mixed pickles, pickling an individual type of vegetable can have advantages. It can help ensure that colors don't bleed to and from other vegetables and taint them. When we make a pickle batch, even though we use various vegetables with different shapes, we aim to keep the ingredients similarly sized. Relatively even-sized pieces mean the pickling can happen evenly and take a similar time to reach maturity.

Sometimes we will use a bit of sugar to balance the sourness of the pickle, but sugar is not a must. We minimize the use of sweeteners when they are not needed, or use only a small amount, so most of our pickles are or can be sugar-free.

You can enjoy your pickles at any stage after making them. The pickle is ready when the vegetables completely absorb the brine and reach their full flavor. Depending on the recipe and the thickness of the cut vegetables, your pickle can be ready within a few days or a few weeks. Test if it is ready by using a clean utensil and taking out a small piece to taste.

Once the pickles are ready to eat, store them in a cool place. A cool pantry in winter is perfect, but on hot summer days it will help to place them in the fridge. Once opened, they should be kept refrigerated in the brine and are best consumed within a few weeks. Pickles that have been removed from the brine will keep in the fridge for up to a week.

Homemade pickles should be expected to last 3–6 months in the pantry or the fridge. If the pickles are pasteurized, they could last up to 2 years. See pages 258–63 for canning instructions.

Equipment

Pickling uses the same equipment as lacto-fermentation (see pages 34–35) with the exception of lids, which for pickling need to be tight. Make sure your lids don't have any exposed metal, as it will react with the vinegar and spoil your pickle.

Pickled Vegetables Middle Eastern Mix

Makes 1.5–2 liters (52–70 fl oz)

The first pickle recipe we want to share is one that is absolutely delicious, easy to make, and can be used to pickle any vegetable. This pickle uses a salt and vinegar brine mixed with a Middle Eastern-style spice mix. The result is a versatile pickle that can be dished out to add crunchy vegetables alongside a wide range of foods. We like to serve it with rice, lentils, meat, and salad or as a snack when enjoying drinks with friends.

2 medium or 3 small onions
¼ medium green cabbage
4 medium carrots
2 bell peppers
1 small cauliflower
100 g (3½ oz) or a small bunch of green beans
6 cloves garlic
Fennel, cucumber, bell pepper, turnips, and asparagus (optional)
5 g (⅛ oz) ground allspice
5 g (⅛ oz) chili powder or 2–3 fresh chilies (use less if preferred)
5 bay leaves

BRINE

20 ml (⅝ fl oz) salt
500 ml (17 fl oz) water
½ cup vinegar
10 g (¼ oz) ground turmeric or 30 g (1 oz) fresh turmeric

Wash and cut the vegetables. Slice the onions into 1 cm (½ in) rings. They don't need to be broken and can stay as compact rings throughout the pickling. Slice the cabbage into strips. Cut the carrots into thin rounds. Slice the bell peppers into strips. Break the cauliflower into florets and slice the cauliflower stem. Remove the ends of the green beans and cut them in half. Slice the garlic cloves or leave whole. Mix the vegetables, allspice, chili, and bay leaves in a large bowl.

Stuff the vegetables and spice mix into a 2 liter (70 fl oz) jar or a few smaller jars if you prefer. The vegetables should be crammed in, leaving just enough room for the brine to get in between them.

For the brine, mix the salt, water, vinegar, and turmeric in a bowl until well combined and the salt has completely dissolved. The brine doesn't need to be heated. Pour the brine mixture over the vegetables. When pouring the brine, you might need to tilt the jar to different angles so that air bubbles can escape. Once full, add a weight and close the jar with a tight lid.

If you need to top up with more brine, add 1½ teaspoons of salt per cup of water and ¼ cup of vinegar.

Ready in 10 days. Store in the pantry for up to 2 months or for longer in the fridge.

Pickled Bell Peppers

Recipe for 1 liter (35 fl oz) jar

This is the recipe Yotam's great-grandma Naima used to make for his grandma, Blanche, when she was a young teenager and "too skinny." This was because pickled bell peppers were Blanche's absolute favorite food, served on a plate of rice with two boiled eggs.

Bell peppers are a very flavorful late-summer and autumn vegetable, and preservation by pickling and minimal flavoring is all that's needed to brighten up a winter day.

This recipe uses the "hot-packing" technique, where vegetables are cooked and then packed into jars. This method removes air from food tissues, shrinks the food, helps keep the food from floating in the jars, and increases the vacuum in the sealed jars, therefore increasing their shelf life. "Hot-packing" allows you to have more vegetables in the same jar compared with "raw-packing." Another advantage of this method is that the color of hot-packed foods will last significantly better over time than raw-packed vegetables.

Variations to this recipe include adding: garlic cloves, dill seeds, or lemon peels. Suggested serving, you guessed it, is with a plate of rice and two boiled eggs.

20–25 small bell peppers (any color)
1 chili, or more to taste

BRINE
2 cups water
1 cup vinegar
15 g (½ oz) salt
1 teaspoon sugar

Check that the bell peppers are clean, whole, and undamaged. Keep the stems if they're still green and look good; otherwise, trim the bell peppers back to the flesh to remove them.

For the brine, mix the water, vinegar, salt, and sugar.

Place the bell peppers and chili in a pan and add the brine, which should cover about two-thirds of the bell peppers. Bring to a boil without a lid, then lower the heat to a simmer and add a lid. Simmer until a bit soft, 15–20 minutes. Depending on the variety used, the bell peppers will likely initially float so while simmering, gently stir to rotate between the ones that are covered and the ones that are poking out of the brine.

Using tongs, transfer the hot bell peppers and chili into a jar. Pour over the cooking brine to cover the bell peppers, place a weight on top, and close the lid. If you are a bit short of brine, make extra brine by boiling together water and vinegar in a 1:1 ratio and adding to the jar.

Will keep in the fridge for 2 months (if you don't devour them first).

Pickled Onions

Recipe for 1 liter (35 fl oz) jar

These crispy onions feel fresh but won't make you cry! The added honey truly enhances the natural sweetness of the onion. We grow pickling onions especially for this purpose because they are small, and many whole onions fit in a jar.

Approx. 25–30 pickling onions (enough to fill a 1 liter/35 fl oz jar)
3 cm (1¼ in) piece fresh ginger
Sprigs of thyme

BRINE
500 ml (17 fl oz) water
250 ml (9 fl oz) vinegar
10 g (¼ oz) honey
5 ml salt

Peel the onions, trim the tops, and make sure the bottom is clean, or cut it off if needed. Pack the onions into the jar tightly. Cut the ginger into small slices and add to the jar with the thyme.

For the brine, combine all the ingredients in a bowl and mix well. Pour the brine over the onions to cover them. Seal the jar, making sure to use a non-metallic lid.

The pickled onions will be ready to eat in 10 days at room temperature, and in about 3 weeks in the fridge. Pickled onions are best stored in the fridge and used within 3 months.

Pickled Olives

Makes 2 liters (70 fl oz)

On Pākaraka Farm, we have a small olive grove of 100 trees. Our farm partners, Harry and the late Jeanette, planted half of it when they bought the farm in the 1990s, and another half about a decade later. Every autumn, we harvest our olives and send them to the local press, just up the valley, to be made into olive oil. When the oil quota for the day is met, we take the time to select some of the bigger olives in the grove to pickle for eating.

There's no better nibble to offer guests than a bowl of farm-grown and home-pickled olives. Getting your yearly supply of table olives is possible even if you don't grow your own trees, as olive trees are sometimes planted for their ornamental value and many go unharvested, whether in parks, backyards, or on streets. Keep your eyes out in olive season (and ask permission from the appropriate people before harvesting).

Fresh olives are bitter and cannot be eaten without treatments. There are various traditional techniques to help remove the bitterness of olives and preserve them for year-round use. We use a three-stage approach, which involves a fairly long period of lacto-fermentation (see stage 2 overleaf). Even though it takes longer than some methods, such as individually cracking each olive, it is, in fact, less labor-intensive while producing outstanding table olives.

Any olive varieties can be pickled, small to large, elliptical or round, with little or more flesh. We recommend using medium to large varieties, such as "Ascolano," "Barnea," "Frantoio," "Kalamata," "Manzanilla," "Picholine," and "Pendolino."

We usually make fairly big batches of olives, multiplying this recipe as needed. Clean, reused food-grade buckets, which usually come in 4 liter (140 fl oz), 10 liter (2.25 gallon), and 20 liter (4.5 gallon) sizes, are great for these larger quantities. Use an inverted plate that fits snugly inside the bucket as a weight.

You can use any size jar to pickle your olives once they are ready for stage 3 (see overleaf). We like spreading our olives between a couple of larger and several smaller jars. The smaller 250–300 ml (9–10½ fl oz) jars are ideal for gifting and it's also a quantity that usually gets eaten in a sitting or within a couple of days. We also use larger 500 ml–1.5 liter (17–52 fl oz) jars, for the sheer beauty of them sitting in these larger vessels, and for a constant supply. These bigger jars can also be opened for a celebratory occasion.

Once a jar is opened, use clean utensils to scoop out to a serving dish. It is best to store the olives in the fridge where they will keep for many more weeks in the brine. Otherwise, consume within a week.

STAGE 1 — WATER TREATMENT

2 liters (70 fl oz) freshly picked olives
Water, enough to cover and replace every day

STAGE 2 — LACTO-FERMENTATION

2 liters (70 fl oz) water-treated olives
Salt, 60 g (2¼ oz) per liter (35 fl oz)
Water, enough to cover as brine

STAGE 3 — PICKLING AND FLAVORING

2 liters (70 fl oz) lacto-fermented olives
Lemon, 2–3 slices per jar
Rosemary, 1 small sprig per jar
Bay leaves, 2 per jar
Allspice, 1–2 per jar
Chilies, 1–2 per jar
Vinegar, ½ cup per liter (35 fl oz) of water in final brine
Salt, 80 g (2¾ oz) per liter (35 fl oz) for final brine
Water, enough to cover
Olive oil

STAGE 1 — WATER TREATMENT

Cover the fresh olives in water, and replace the water on a daily basis for 7 days. When making large quantities, we usually do this in a tub that allows easy draining and refilling. The water treatment is the first tool in our box for getting rid of the bitterness of the olives. But each time we replace the water, we also lose some of the flavor of the olives. That's why we usually limit the water treatment to 7 days.

STAGE 2 — LACTO-FERMENTATION

Move the olives to a jar or bucket, and cover with brine made with salt and water at a ratio of 60 g (2¼ oz) salt for every liter (35 fl oz) of water. Let the olives sit in this brine for a minimum of 2 months. Keep the olives fully submerged under the brine.

STAGE 3 — PICKLING AND FLAVORING

Drain the olives from the stage 2 brine and rinse lightly.

Pack the olives into jars in layers, occasionally interchanging with slices of lemon, rosemary, bay leaves, allspice, and chilies, up to 1 cm (½ in) below the rim of the jar.

Make the pickling brine by bringing 1 liter (35 fl oz) of water to a boil with ½ cup vinegar and 80 g (2¾ oz) salt. Depending on the size of your olives and how tightly they're packed, this should cover olives spread across multiple jars.

Pour the hot brine over the packed olives to keep the ingredients covered. Place a tablespoon of olive oil at the top of each jar to seal the olives in and protect them. Ready in 1 week.

Turnips Iraqi-style

Makes 2 liters (70 fl oz)

Another great recipe from Yotam's grandma, Blanche, which originated from her birth country, Iraq. Iraq has a rich fermenting, preserving, and pickling culture that goes far back in history and is reflected in the variety of pickles in its cuisine. When growing up, Yotam's family met every weekend for an extended family meal with aunties and cousins. At Yotam's grandma's house in Tel Aviv, these pickled turnips were a regular dish, accompanied by tbit (chicken with rice) and many types of pickles and salads.

This is an easy recipe to make and a great way to use turnips and create delicious pickles. A highlight of this pickle is the beautiful color—light to vibrant pink (see photo on page 91). This tasty snack or side dish is crunchy, salty, and sour. So good.

Serve as a starter, in sandwiches and, of course, as part of a chicken, rice, and vegetables meal.

Approx. 1 kg/2 lb 4 oz turnips (2–3 large turnips)
1 medium beet

BRINE
10 g (¼ oz) salt
2 cups water
1 cup vinegar

Peel the turnips and beet, and cut them into sticks 1 cm (½ in) thick. In a bowl, mix the turnips and beet and pack them tightly in the jar. Leave room for slices of beet to go at the top.

Prepare the brine by mixing all the ingredients well.

Add the brine to the jar, and place a weight on the beet. You can try using one large beet slice and wedge it at the top so it acts as a weight.

The pickled turnips will be ready to eat in 3 days at room temperature or in 7 days in the fridge. Best stored in the fridge and used within 2 months.

Trouble-shooting for Pickles

How to know if the pickle has spoiled

A pickle has gone bad if it has been contaminated, which will not be difficult to recognize. This could be a visible mold or a rancid smell that is distinctly different from the sour-smelling good-to-eat vinegar.

Always use at least the minimum amount of vinegar and salt; if they are too low, yeast will be able to proliferate and can spoil your pickles. If you want to add extra vinegar and salt, that's all right.

In any case of doubt, it is best to discard the whole jar and not just scrape off the bad-looking part.

Garlic has turned blue-green

There is a surprising phenomenon that is specific to garlic being exposed to acids, such as lemon juice and vinegar. In the acidic conditions of the pickle brine, the tiny residual amounts of copper in the vinegar or water can react with sulphur compounds in the garlic cloves and, through an enzymatic process, turn them to varying shades of blue and green. Using fresh garlic will reduce the chance of this happening, but in any case it is not harmful to eat the garlic or any other parts of the pickle.

The brine is cloudy or murky

Cloudy or murky brine doesn't by itself mean that the pickle has been spoiled. It can be caused by lactic acid bacteria, using salt containing anti-caking agents, using hard water with a high mineral content, or mushy vegetables. If the pickle is free of mold and smells good, it should be safe to eat and doesn't need to be discarded. In case of mushy vegetables, rather than throwing the pickle away you can use it instead of vinegar to flavor soups, marinate meats, and make salad dressings.

Avoid pickles becoming soft

Use fresh, crisp vegetables. If the vegetables start to soften before pickling, a soak in ice-cold water will bring them back to crispness. Place cold water and ice in a bowl or food-grade container, and submerge the vegetables for a few hours before making pickles.

For cucumbers, scraping off the flower scar at the bottom end will reduce enzymatic softening.

Adding bay leaves or grape leaves, which are tannin-rich, will also help keep vegetables crisp (see page 37).

When pasteurizing pickles (see page 20), to keep the vegetables crisper you can pasteurize them at a lower temperature. Pasteurizing at a lower temperature but over a longer time will be just as effective as high-heat, short pasteurization, such as a duration of 30 minutes at 82°C (180°F).

Kombucha, Jun & Ginger Beer

Kombucha is a fermented drink made from a sweetened tea together with a kombucha symbiotic culture of bacteria and yeast (SCOBY), which converts sugar into carbon and acid.

Kombucha has steadily grown in popularity, and it is now common and readily available commercially. Commercial kombucha is often diluted and artificially carbonated, so be ready for your homebrewed versions to taste a bit different from the ones in the shop.

Jun is pretty much the same as kombucha, with the important exception that it grows in a honey-sweetened brew.

Homemade kombucha and jun are easy to make with great flavor combinations.

Ginger beer has been a long-time favorite in many parts of the world, and we love making and drinking it. We make it using a yeasty ginger bug starter, easily made at home. For most of this chapter we will concentrate on kombucha and jun, and toward the end it will be time for ginger beer to shine.

Ingredients & equipment for kombucha & jun

Let's explore the key components to better understand their roles in making refreshing kombucha and jun.

Sugar

Sugar is food for the microorganisms in the SCOBY. A variety of sugar sources can be used to make kombucha; however, we find that each sugar source also adds a distinct flavor that can become very dominant in the drink. Our preference is to use organic golden cane sugar for kombucha, which doesn't impact the overall flavor as much as alternatives and provides consistent results.

Honey

The sugar source of choice for jun is honey. We use local bush honey from the farm and valley. Different sources of honey will affect the brew's flavor, making this another fun aspect you might want to experiment with.

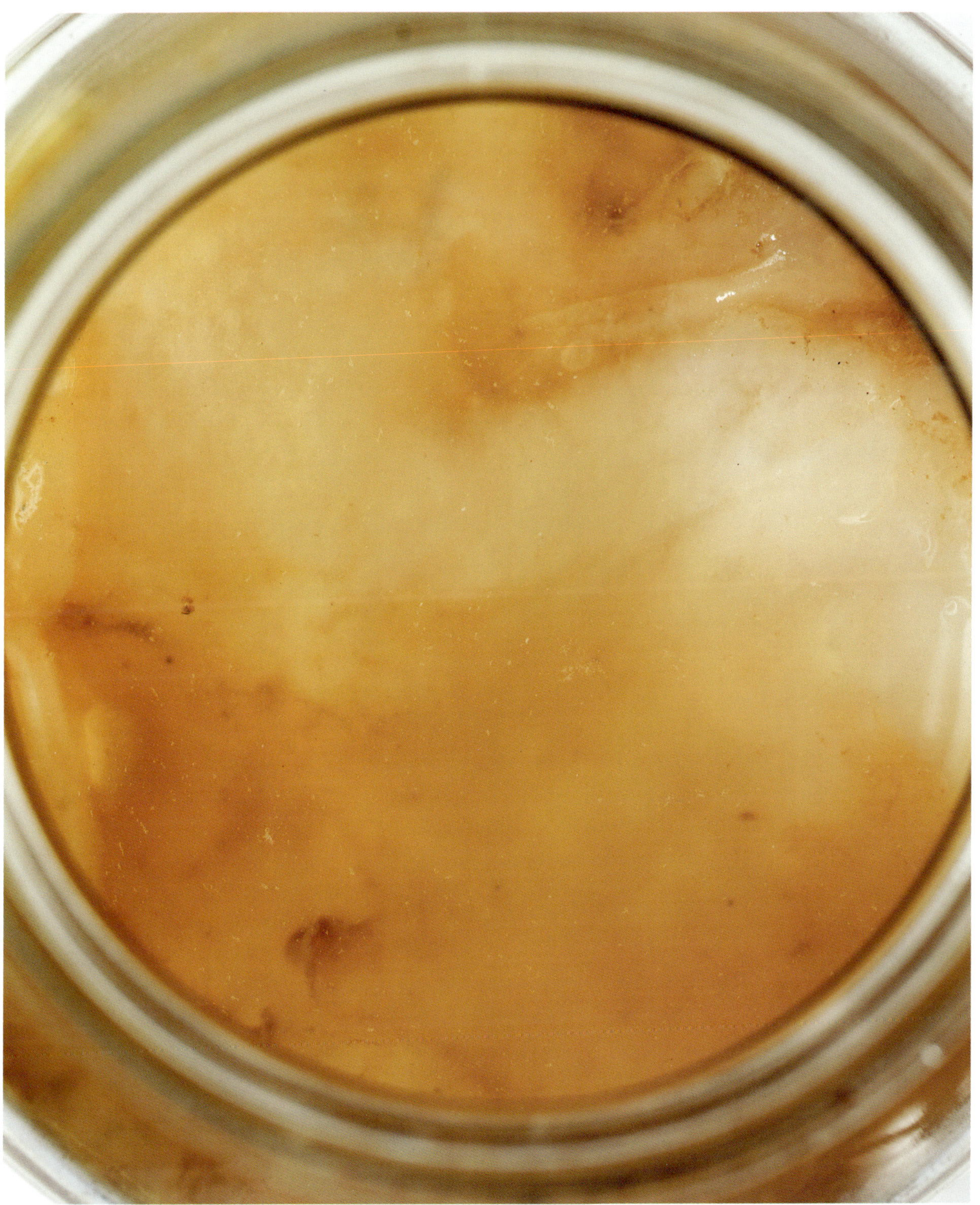

Tea

Kombucha is traditionally made with black tea and commonly with other teas from the plant *Camellia sinensis* (green, white, oolong, etc.). However, kombucha can be just as successfully made using a variety of herbal teas, as well as fruit.*

During kombucha fermentation, the bioactive compounds content in the drink increases compared with the pre-fermentation brew (with most but not all herbal tea or fruit substrates). The type of herb or fruit used in the brew determines which bioactive compounds—such as organic acids, antioxidants, soluble vitamins, and essential minerals, many of which have health benefits—will be present in the end beverage. For example, kombucha made from lemon balm has a higher antioxidant content than black tea kombucha.†

Our current SCOBY came from our friend Sarah who had been brewing her kombucha using rooibos tea for a couple of years prior. It easily took on all the other herbal tea brews we have been making it with.

If experimenting with new brews, we recommend always having a backup SCOBY growing in the substance it is most used to. It is also a good practice to keep separate lineages of SCOBY, as they adapt to your preference combinations.

In this chapter, we share our favorite brews, using teas, herbs, and more.

Acid

For your SCOBY community to stay healthy and avoid mold development, it needs an initial acidity of under pH 5. This is achieved by backslopping—adding mature kombucha/jun to every new brew. If backslopping is not an option, adding natural vinegar at a ratio of 40 ml (1¼ fl oz) per liter (35 fl oz) will do the trick.

Backslopping will obviously affect the flavor of your brew. We try to maintain lines of same-flavored brews, backslopping from one to the next, or at least consider a good combination when that is not an option.

Insufficient acidity is one of the leading causes of failed brews and moldy SCOBY, and is the first thing we check for if anything seems to be going wrong.

---

* S. A. Villarreal-Soto, S. Beaufort, J. Bouajila, J-P. Souchard and P. Taillandier, "Understanding Kombucha Tea Fermentation: A Review," *Journal of Food Science* 83 (2018): 580–588. https://doi.org/10.1111/1750-3841.14068.

† Bruna Milena Bortolomedi, Camila Souza Paglarini and Fábio Cristiano Angonesi Brod, "Bioactive Compounds in Kombucha: A Review of Substrate Effect and Fermentation Conditions," *Food Chemistry* 385 (15 August 2022): 132719, https://doi.org/10.1016/j.foodchem.2022.132719.

SCOBY

To brew kombucha and jun, you need to start with their respective SCOBYs. As SCOBYs multiply, if you know anyone already making kombucha or jun, they would likely be more than happy to share a SCOBY with you. You can also buy a SCOBY online or start one from a store-bought raw kombucha.

A new SCOBY is formed every time you brew your kombucha or jun. This new SCOBY either grows as a new layer on your current one, or sometimes as an independent SCOBY floating by itself. You can use the thicker SCOBY in your next batch and, over time, discard the older layers to maintain a SCOBY in a size that is easy to work with. You can separate the SCOBY into layers or cut it to make separate brews. An exponential number of separate brews is possible, each with its own unique teas and herbs. And, of course, now you too can share the love by offering SCOBYs to keen friends and neighbors.

The SCOBY needs to remain moist to be healthy. Sometimes during the fermentation process your SCOBY can be pushed up from the surface of the brew. If this happens, push it back down.

Always handle your SCOBY with clean hands to avoid contamination.

Finally, if your SCOBY has gone moldy, it is not sufficient to just discard the moldy part. Get rid of the SCOBY and the brew it was in, as it is unsafe to drink. Make sure to sanitize your container before using it again.

Resting your SCOBY

If you are planning to take a break from brewing, leave your SCOBY in a freshly made brew following the regular kombucha recipe. Top up with new tea every couple of months, and take this opportunity to check for mold. You can store multiple SCOBYs together in this way, in a practice known as a "SCOBY hotel," where vacationing SCOBYs hang out.

Keep an eye on your resting SCOBYs in case they push out of the brew, in which case push them back in.

Containers

Kombucha and jun should be brewed in clean wide-mouth containers to allow the SCOBY a good surface area to grow in. It should not be brewed in metal or plastic, which can react to the acidic environment. We brew ours in 1, 2 and 4 liter (35, 70 and 140 fl oz) glass jars.

The first fermentation of kombucha and jun is aerobic; this means that the containers need to be covered with cloth or fine mesh to allow the SCOBY access to oxygen but stop insects and other contaminants from getting in.

Black Tea Kombucha

Recipe for 1 liter (35 fl oz) jar

A SCOBY, a couple of tea bags from the pantry, and sugar are all you need to get started with brewing your own classic kombucha.

We love trying out different blends of tea—it is incredible how much variation this gives in the final drink. We like a strong brew of English Breakfast for a full-bodied kombucha. We also really enjoy using the floral-tasting oolong tea, which sits between black and green tea, for a refreshing, light brew. Our friend Shai mixes green and black 50–50 in his brews to get them to just the way he likes.

Black Tea Kombucha is great on its own or as a base for flavoring in second fermentation (see page 100).

850 ml (29 fl oz) boiling water
⅓ cup sugar
15 ml (½ fl oz) loose tea or 2 tea bags (we use organic black tea or organic oolong tea)
125 ml (4 fl oz) mature kombucha (or 40 ml (1¼ fl oz) natural vinegar)
Kombucha SCOBY

Boil 1–2 cups of the water and mix in the sugar and tea, stirring until the sugar dissolves. Cover and steep for about 10 minutes. Strain the sweetened tea into a wide glass container. Add the remaining water that was not boiled—this should cool your tea quickly.

Once the tea is at room temperature, add the mature kombucha liquid and the SCOBY. Cover the container tightly with a clean cloth and a rubber band.

The kombucha will be ready in 7–12 days—age for your desired acidity. In the summer, we start checking readiness after 7 days, and in other seasons a couple of days later. Twenty-four hours make a big difference in kombucha brewing, so even if the brew is too sweet today, recheck it tomorrow.

Separate the SCOBY and set aside enough mature brew to acidify your next batch. Strain the remaining kombucha and pour into jars or bottles. The kombucha brew is ready to drink straight away.

For a more fizzy kombucha and to add additional flavors, continue to the second fermentation (see page 100).

Second Fermentation

The second fermentation is the process that happens when the mature kombucha brew, without the SCOBY, is placed in an airtight container such as a tight-lid bottle. During this process, the remaining sugars are transformed into carbon dioxide (CO_2), naturally carbonating the drink as they cannot escape through the tight lid.

We usually allow our kombucha to carbonate in clean flip-top bottles for 4–5 days in a cool spot in the house before enjoying it or transferring it to the fridge.

If you plan to bottle your kombucha without adding additional sweetening, it's best to do so while the brew is still a little sweet, so try to catch it a little earlier (a day is plenty) than you would for drinking it straight.

It's important to remember that too much carbonation can lead to intense pressure building up in the bottles. This build-up can lead to a large portion of your brew bubbling out like Champagne upon opening or, in the worst case, to the whole bottle exploding.

To mitigate these risks, be calculated with how much fruit, fresh or dry, and any other sugars you add to your second fermentation process; a little goes a long way. Use round bottles that can handle pressure over square or angular bottles. And, if you are planning to keep bottles for an extended period outside of the fridge, "burp" them occasionally by opening the lid for a moment to release some of the CO_2. Finally, open your kombucha bottles over the sink with a cup ready at hand in case things get wild.

Kombucha, like other yeasty ferments, naturally contains a low level of alcohol, from about 0.2 percent. Depending on temperature, time, surface area, and type of tea it can be higher than the legal threshold of 0.5 percent, with some researchers measuring about 1, 2 and in white and red tea even 3 percent.* Second fermentation increases the alcohol level a little, as the yeast continues to break down the sugars in the brew.

---

* C. W. Sandor, "Alcohol Content of Kombucha: A Review of Literature," *Journal of the International Society of Beverage Technologists* 7, no. 3 (September 2009): 521.

Raspberry Leaf & Lemon Geranium Kombucha

Recipe for 1 liter (35 fl oz) jar

We grow a few varieties of geranium in our garden hedges. These beautiful plants grow BIG and spread out. They look great as greenery in a flower bouquet and are nice for flavoring water on a hot day; however, we don't have many other uses for them. That's why we were so pleased to find they make wonderful kombuchas. Lemon geranium kombucha tastes like old-fashioned lemonade, especially after the second fermentation. The raspberry leaf adds depth of flavor, high healthy phytochemical contents,* and extra tannins. This is the one kombucha we always have going, making 4 liters (140 fl oz) at a time, and it's never enough to keep up with the demand.

850 ml (29 fl oz) water
⅓ cup sugar
5 g (⅛ oz) raspberry leaf
5 g (⅛ oz) lemon geranium leaf (or more)
125 ml (4 fl oz) mature kombucha (or 40 ml [1¼ fl oz] natural vinegar)
Kombucha SCOBY

Boil 1–2 cups of the water and mix in the sugar and herbal leaves, stirring until the sugar dissolves. Cover and steep for at least 20 minutes. Strain the sweetened tea into a wide glass container. Add the remaining water that was not boiled—this should cool your tea quickly.

Once the tea is at room temperature, add the mature kombucha liquid and the SCOBY. Cover the container tightly with a cloth and a rubber band.

The kombucha will be ready in 7–12 days—age for your desired acidity. We recommend bottling for second fermentation (see page 100) to really get the best result from this recipe.

* Ting Luo, et al., "Phytochemical Composition and Potential Biological Activities Assessment of Raspberry Leaf Extracts from Nine Different Raspberry Species and Raspberry Leaf Tea," *Journal of Berry Research* 10, no. 2 (1 January 2020): 295–309, https://doi.org/10.3233/JBR-190474.

Apple Mint Kombucha

Recipe for 1 liter (35 fl oz) jar

Apple mint grows all around us; it is a weed that has spread wildly in our area. That means that we have an abundant supply within easy reach. Turns out it makes amazing kombucha, which is extra refreshing when turned to ice blocks (see page 107).

850 ml (29 fl oz) water
⅓ cup sugar
15 g (½ oz) fresh apple mint leaves
125 ml (4 fl oz) mature kombucha (or 40 ml [1¼ fl oz] natural vinegar)
Kombucha SCOBY

Boil 1–2 cups of the water and mix in the sugar and apple mint leaves, stirring until the sugar dissolves. Cover and steep for at least 20 minutes. Strain the sweetened tea into a wide glass container. Add the remaining water that was not boiled—this should cool your tea quickly.

Once the tea is at room temperature, add the mature kombucha liquid and the SCOBY. Cover the container tightly with a clean cloth and a rubber band.

The kombucha will be ready in 7–12 days—age for your desired acidity.

Apple Mint Kombucha Ice Blocks

Kombucha, jun, and ginger beer all make great ice blocks. When we were little, we used to make ice blocks in cups, balancing spoons between two rubber bands to keep them centerd. Now reusable ice block molds are easy to get in both classic and various fun shapes. We enjoy being creative with them, adding sliced fruit, edible flowers such as viola, cornflowers, rose and dahlia petals, spices, and even cucumber and greens such as sorrel and fennel to the mix. Add-ons such as fruit should be packed tightly. Lightweight additions, such as very small flower petals, will float to the top (which will end up at the bottom), so don't add too many.

Thin slices of cucumber
Dahlia petals* (you can trim the bottom tips if you don't like their slightly bitter flavor)
Ready-to-drink Apple Mint Kombucha (see page 104)

Using your preferred mold, start by filling it with the cucumber slices, 2–4 slices per ice block, depending on your mold.

Fit in the dahlia petals around the cucumber slices. We grow fairly big dahlias, with some petals as long as the length of the whole ice block that can be arranged side by side. Smaller petals can be stacked in layers.

Once you are happy with your ingredient combination, gently pour in the kombucha, add the sticks/handle, and freeze. Ready in approx. 5 hours depending on how cold your freezer is.

Fun fact: pink and purple dahlias are higher in protein, fiber, and (alongside cherry-colored flowers) also higher in vitamin C and flavonoids than other colors that were tested.

---

* María Teresa Martínez-Damián, et al., "Nutritional Value, Bioactive Compounds and Capacity Antioxidant in Edible Flowers of Dahlia," *Acta Scientiarum Polonorum Hortorum Cultus* 20, no. 5 (29 October 2021): 63–72, https://doi.org/10.24326/asphc.2021.5.6.

Jun

Jun uses a SCOBY similar to kombucha, adapted specifically to ferment honey tea. The preparation follows the same process as kombucha, just substituting the SCOBY with a jun SCOBY, and the sugar with honey.

Jun ferments quicker than kombucha and can be ready in 3–5 days in the same environment, whereas kombucha takes about 10 days.

Jun is often made with green tea but, like kombucha, can also be made with herbs instead of tea. We have found that herbal jun can be ready in as quickly as 2 days, and trying various herbs has provided reliable results. We particularly like mint jun (see opposite) and it's also lovely made with lemon balm with a bit of basil. Ultimately every herb that works for kombucha also works with jun. This is exciting for us as with local honey and garden herbs, jun allows us to make a fully farm-grown fizzy drink.

Things to take into account when brewing jun:

- Jun is a very active brew that needs more frequent burping than kombucha to avoid explosions. Bottled jun is ready to drink after 1–2 days. Use strong bottles and check them regularly if you are not drinking them soon after bottling.
- Jun, like kombucha, contains naturally occurring alcohol, usually in small amounts. We have found that when making jun with added fruit, it can develop a higher than usual alcohol content in the first fermentation within 2–3 days. This is important to be aware of especially if avoiding alcohol is important in your life.

Just Mint Jun

Recipe for 1 liter (35 fl oz) jar

This is a house favorite. It's great on its own straight from the first batch or mixed in with anything that can use a bit of mint.

We like to make our mint brew pretty strong. We use fresh mint from the garden and often use 50 g (1¾ oz) and upward for our 2 liter (70 fl oz) batches. We also tend to leave the mint in for a longer steep time, an hour or more. Use this recipe with any other herb, replacing the mint with 20 g (¾ oz) of fresh herbs or 15 g (½ oz) of dry herbs.

850 ml (29 fl oz) water
⅓ cup honey
20 g (¾ oz) fresh garden mint or 15 g (½ oz) dry mint
125 ml (4 fl oz) mature mint jun (or 40 ml (1¼ fl oz) vinegar)
Jun SCOBY

Boil 2 cups of the water and mix in the honey and mint, stirring until the honey dissolves. Cover and steep for 10 minutes or more. Strain the mint brew into a wide glass container. Add the remaining water that was not boiled—this should cool your mint brew quickly.

Once the brew is at room temperature, remove the mint and add the mature jun and SCOBY. Cover the container tightly with a clean cloth and rubber band.

Ready in 2–5 days. Drink as is, or bottle for a second fermentation (see page 100).

Jun is a very active brew that needs more frequent burping than kombucha to avoid explosions. ***Use strong bottles and check them regularly.***

Mint Jun Cocktail

Serves 2

Kombucha and jun make fantastic cocktail ingredients. Kombucha and gin has long been a house favorite, but mint jun, in our opinion, trumps them all. This is a fun little cocktail to enjoy on a sunny weekend with friends. Mint is the leading flavor with clean good-quality vodka for a little extra kick.

Ice, to fill the cup
120 ml (4 fl oz) fresh or frozen raspberries
80 ml (2½ fl oz) vodka
40 ml (1¼ fl oz) Beet Kvass (see page 51)
40 ml (1¼ fl oz) freshly squeezed lemon juice
200 ml (7 fl oz) bottled Just Mint Jun (see page 109)
Fresh mint leaves, to garnish

Fill two cups with ice and raspberries. Divide the vodka, Beet Kvass, and lemon juice between the cups. Open a bottle of fizzy mint jun and pour on an angle into each cup. Adding the jun last will maintain the most fizz.

Garnish and enjoy!

Green Tea Jun

Recipe for 1 liter (35 fl oz) jar

850 ml (29 fl oz) water
⅓ cup honey
15 ml (½ fl oz) loose green tea or 2 tea bags
100 ml (3½ fl oz) mature jun (or 40 ml (1¼ fl oz) vinegar)
Jun SCOBY

Boil 1–2 cups of the water and mix in the honey and green tea, stirring until the honey dissolves. Cover and steep for 5 minutes. Strain the sweetened tea into a wide glass container. Add the remaining water that was not boiled—this should cool your tea quickly.

Once the brew is at room temperature add the mature jun and SCOBY. Cover the container tightly with a clean cloth and rubber band.

Check for readiness after 3 days and recheck daily until you like the level of sourness. After brewing, jun can be put through a second fermentation the same way as kombucha (see page 100), again needing a shorter duration of 1–2 days.

Jun is a very active brew that needs more frequent burping than kombucha to avoid explosions. *Use strong bottles and check them regularly.*

Lemon balm
Basil
Jun 21/9
Gamboot 11/9
Rose Geranium leaves
lavender tip + flower
cardamom Pods x 3
Nettle Jun
21/9
Black tea + date
19/9 kombucha
Gumboot & Sage
9/9
Fennel
Gumboot 22/9
kombucha

Mint Jun
23/9
Green tea
Jun
19/9
Green tea 24/9
Jun
+ strawberry
Green tea 15/9
Jun
+ 2 cherries

Trouble-shooting for Kombucha & Jun

Mold growth on the SCOBY

If mold is present on your SCOBY, you will have to discard the SCOBY and the brew. Sanitize the vessel before reusing. The most common reason for mold growth is not enough acidity in the original brew. Make sure to always backslop mature brew into the new batch, or supplement with vinegar if that is not possible. While the quick acidification of kombucha means that starting with a pH of 5 should normally be fine, some sources recommend starting at pH 4.6 or lower to avoid any chance of contamination on the very first day of brewing. You can use a pH strip to measure the pH of your brew quickly and easily. Add more mature brew or vinegar as necessary to drop the pH down.

SCOBY is not growing

Certain substances, such as essential oils, preservatives, and artificial flavoring, can be harmful to the SCOBY, so always use natural teas in your brew. If your SCOBY continues to not thrive, try a different tea or adjust the sugar level. Too much sugar can harm the SCOBY, and too little won't provide enough nutrition. Remember to keep a backup SCOBY when experimenting with new substrates. While kombucha tastes best to us while it is still sweet, the SCOBY continues to feed many days and even weeks later, so set a SCOBY in a SCOBY hotel (see page 97) and see if with time it is recovering. Finally, a SCOBY doesn't like to be moved around so, as much as possible, leave your brew where it is and let the new SCOBY form peacefully.

The brew is acidic

There are a couple of reasons that can lead to this. The first is just an issue of time; try catching the brew a couple of days earlier, and recheck regularly. Sometimes the difference is between it being a bit too sweet in the morning and perfect by evening.

The second reason is not enough sugar in the brew, especially if your SCOBY is very big. Try increasing the amount of sugar slightly and reducing the size of your SCOBY.

Finally, if you are backslopping mature brew that is also too sour, your brew is off to an acidic start. And if every batch comes out too sour, you are in a loop of sourness. In this case, think of your mature brew as you would vinegar and reduce the amount of backslop accordingly.

Dealing with insects

When fruit flies are in season, it is important to use a tight cloth on top of your brew. The flies are very small and are capable of laying eggs through normal cheesecloth. Either use multiple layers or a tight-woven cloth to stop a maggot infection on your SCOBY. If we have a serious infection of flies in the brew, we discard the whole thing.

Another problem is ants—attracted to the sweetness of the brew, they crawl in and drown to death. When ants are an issue, we stop them from crawling in by placing our jars in a water dish that acts as a barrier. Ants that have made it into the brew sometimes get incorporated into the SCOBY. You can remove them by peeling or cutting off those parts of the SCOBY.

The brew is too fizzy

If your bottled brews always bubble away when you open them, they might be too sugary at the time of bottling, so try waiting a little longer before bottling. Alternatively keep your bottled brews in the fridge to slow down the yeast activity. If your bottles are sitting on the shelf a while, try burping regularly. Some flavoring added in the bottling stage can also increase fizziness, especially fruit. If you are flavoring at this stage, try using herbs instead of fruit and spices.

The brew is too flat

A flat brew is usually the result of insufficient sugar, which the yeast feed on, creating carbonation. Try upping the sugar content or trying a new type of sugar. When bottling, catch your brew a day earlier than how you would like to drink it unbottled, leaving enough sugar for carbonation to take place in the bottle.

If your brew was fine before bottling and then turned flat and/or sour, your lids might not be tight enough. Try a flip-top bottle and make sure the seals are intact. If the lids are tight but the weather is cold, it might also just be taking longer, so try waiting another few days before opening your bottles. Finally, consider adding to your bottle extra sugar, or a bit of fruit, juice, ginger, or cardamom.

Homemade Ginger Beer

Our first encounter with real homemade ginger beer was in a West African restaurant in Paris, France, in 2007. The richness of the drink blew us away. Since then, every so often we remember the richness and yumminess of homemade ginger beer and we're tempted to make another batch.

The recipe we use to make this drink uses a dedicated "ginger bug." It is a bit of a ritual to make the ginger bug, but it is very simple. The ginger bug is surprisingly versatile and can be used to introduce yeasts in other recipes for making drinks and bakes.

At some point in our ginger beer–making journey we asked ourselves, why not try making it with honey (our go-to sweetener) rather than sugar? Well, we did, and guess what? It tasted great! For the past few years, we have made most of our ginger beer with honey, which is included in the recipe here, but you can use it interchangeably with sugar. We do use sugar when making the ginger bug.

We have also used ginger bugs to make beautiful loaves of bread instead of a sourdough starter. An active ginger bug is especially useful when there isn't an active sourdough starter available. When your ginger bug is going, try making a bread loaf. Use one of the loaf recipes in the sourdough chapter (see pages 164–90), but substitute the sourdough starter with an equivalent amount of strained ginger bug liquid.

We started using ginger bugs to ferment juices and other liquids a few years ago. Most of what we made was delicious and refreshing. These drinks can be an enticing gateway to get others to enjoy fermented drinks. While we have made some funky (and yummy) drinks by leaving the bug in for several weeks, a few days of fermenting juice produces a gently fermented soft drink. For some inspiration, see the recipes that follow Ginger Beer.

Ginger bug maintenance

You can keep your ginger bug jar at room temperature and feed it with even amounts of sugar and ginger daily. This way, your bug will stay healthy, potent, and ready for use. If you only plan on making a single batch and don't have any immediate uses for the bug, you can feed it and then keep it in the fridge for up to a month with a closed lid. We usually keep a bit of ginger bug in the fridge, and when needed, reactivate it and make another ginger beer batch. You can also freeze your ginger bug and reactivate it before you want to use it. Alternatively, as it is so easy to make again, prepare a new bug when you are ready to make a new ginger beer batch.

Ginger Bug Starter

The key to making bubbly-rich ginger beer is making the microbes come alive, feasting on ginger and sugar in what's referred to as the "ginger bug." Once the ginger bug is bubbly, we brew a sweet ginger tea, let it cool down, add a bit of lemon juice, and the ginger bug, and bottle it all up. So easy and so good.

Making a ginger bug will be a process that spreads over a few days and up to a week, but it probably will not take you more than 10 minutes throughout that time.

For this recipe, you will need a wide jar of over 400 ml (14 fl oz) to make the ginger bug, and another small jar to keep the finely cut or grated ginger to feed the ginger bug in.

We tried making the ginger bug starter with honey instead of sugar a few times, but it wasn't as smooth and quick. We prefer and recommend using sugar and not honey to start and feed the ginger bug.

10 cm (4 in, 60–80 g/2¼–2¾ oz) piece fresh ginger, skin on and trimmed of any mold

5–9 teaspoons sugar

1 cup water

Chop or grate the ginger finely. Take 2 teaspoons of the finely grated or cut fresh ginger and place it in a large wide jar (400 ml/14 fl oz or more). Place the remaining ginger in a small jar in the fridge. You will be using it over the coming few days.

Add 2 teaspoons of the sugar to the jar and top it up with the water. Stir the mixture until the sugar is dissolved, and cover it tightly with a clean cloth so flies can't get in. Place the jar in a warm spot out of direct sunlight but in a highly visible place, which will help you remember it.

As much as there is nothing mystical about this process, for a measure of good luck and a bit of fun, we make a silent invitation (or, if one of our kids is around, Yotam will make an exaggerated loud one) for the ginger beer-loving yeast to enjoy this feast.

Over the next few days, once a day (twice is even better, but don't feel pressured), add 1 teaspoon of grated ginger from the small jar and 1 teaspoon of sugar into the big jar and stir vigorously. This helps increase the oxygen levels in the jar and remove any film that might develop at the top.

Depending on the type of yeast, the temperature, and those ginger bug spirits, you will notice the contents of the jar become bubbly within 1 day to a week. When the bubbles start, that indicates it is ready. We usually expect bubbling to happen within 3–5 days, but in recent years we made several new ginger bugs that started bubbling in less than 24 hours and made an excellent fizzy brew.

Ginger Beer

Makes 4 liters (140 fl oz)

As mentioned, we now use honey when making our ginger beer, but most sugars will work, so you can use what you have at home. We prefer full-bodied raw sugars, which give the drink a darker look and additional flavors.

4 liters (140 fl oz) water
5–15 cm (2–6 in) piece fresh ginger, skin on and trimmed of any mold
1½ cups honey or sugar
Juice of 2 lemons
1 cup Ginger Bug Starter (see page 119)

Pour 2 liters (70 fl oz) of the water into a large pot. Grate the fresh ginger or finely chop it. Use about 5 cm (2 in, 30–40 g/1–1½ oz) of fresh ginger for a mild-flavored drink, 10 cm (4 in, 60–80 g/2¼–2¾ oz) for an excellent standard drink, and up to 15 cm (6 in, 90–120 g/3¼–4¼ oz) for an intense ginger flavor. Add the fresh ginger, and bring the brew to a boil.

When we have no further use for the ginger bug, or simply a large quantity of it, we add the excess ginger bug to the pot and cook it together with the fresh ginger. If it is a substantial amount, reduce the amount of fresh ginger to compensate.

Once boiling, reduce the heat to a simmer and cook for 15 minutes. Let the sweet ginger brew cool down to under 40°C (105°F). Once the brew has cooled down, you can add the rest of the ingredients to the pot: honey or sugar (if using sugar, it can be added at the same time as the ginger), lemon juice, and the ginger bug, and mix well. You can tip in all the contents in your ginger bug jar, or pour in just the liquid and keep the ginger.

Once the honey or sugar has completely dissolved, top it up to 4 liters (140 fl oz) of water.

Before bottling, you will need to strain the suspended particles in the brew. One option is to fit a small sieve over a funnel to catch the ginger as you pour the brew into bottles.

Don't discard the ginger yet, as the strained ginger is still potent and flavorful. We got into the habit of using it once more by making chai.

It is essential to use bottles that can handle the pressure that will form during the carbonation stage. Flip-top bottles made for beer-making work best. Other glass bottles with a tight lid and plastic bottles are okay to use, but it is essential to "burp" them often and regularly until the fermentation decreases.

Keep the brew in the bottles for about 2 weeks at room temperature. After 2 weeks, transfer your ginger beer to the fridge. It is ready now and will keep well. It is best drunk cold, and it will definitely fizz, so open it carefully away from anyone's face, over a sink.

Apple Juice Ginger Bug Soda

Makes 1 liter (35 fl oz)

One of the simplest ways to use a ginger bug is to add it to any fruit juice and let it do its thing. Try this recipe to ferment apple juice into a delicious fermented drink.

1 liter (35 fl oz) apple juice

1 tablespoon Ginger Bug Starter (see page 119)

Transfer the juice to a wide jar, or use the same bottle the drink came with. Add the ginger bug and mix well. Place a cloth on top of the jar and secure it with a string or a rubber band.

Mix daily and brew the ferment for 3 days for a gentle flavor and up to 10 days for a funkier brew.

Transfer the brew to a bottle, preferably a flip-top, close the lid, and let it ferment for 1–2 weeks. It is a good idea to burp the bottle every few days to check on the fermentation and release any extra pressure. Instead of transferring the brew to a bottle, you could also keep it under an airlock for this fermentation stage and then bottle it.

Transfer to the fridge and drink cold.

Strawberry Ginger Bug Soda

Makes 1 liter (35 fl oz)

We make many delicious berry sodas with the ginger bug. They are very easy to make, and you can use any berry you like for this recipe.

1 cup fresh or frozen strawberries
1 tablespoon honey or sugar
About 3 cups water
1 tablespoon Ginger Bug Starter (see page 119)

Place the strawberries, honey or sugar, and water in a blender and blend until the texture is smooth. Add about 1 tablespoon of ginger bug and mix briefly.

Transfer the brew to a wide jar, place a cloth on top, and secure it.

Mix daily and brew the ferment for 3 days for a gentle flavor and up to 10 days for a funkier brew.

Transfer the brew to a bottle, preferably a flip-top, close the lid, and let it ferment for 1–2 weeks. It is a good idea to burp the bottle after a day to check on the fermentation and release extra pressure and again in the next few days. Transfer to the fridge and drink cold.

Trouble-shooting for Ginger Beer

When the ginger bug stops bubbling

If you keep your ginger bug alive, fed, and happy after making a ginger beer batch, over time you might notice that the bug stops being bubbly after feeding. This is easily fixed by diluting the ginger bug starter with water. We suggest taking a tablespoon from your starter and transferring it to another jar with 1 teaspoon of fresh ginger, 1 teaspoon of sugar, and 1 cup of water.

You can use the excess of your ginger bug starter in your next ginger beer brew during the boiling stage to lessen the need for fresh ginger. Alternatively, you can strain the ginger and pour the liquid into ice cubes. Once frozen, the ice cubes can be transferred to a bag or container and be used as needed as a basis for future ginger beer starters.

Alcohol content in ginger beer

The ginger beer recipe we include here (on page 120) will not make a strong alcoholic drink. Reducing the honey or sugar content will reduce the alcohol content even further. Your brew will likely end up with 0.5 percent to 1.5 percent alcohol, similar to homemade jun.

Storing ginger beer

If you plan to store your ginger beer for a while, keep it in the fridge. In the fridge, the fermentation will continue but much slower. The longer the bottled ginger beer sits in the fridge, the "drier" and less sweet it will become. We haven't kept ours for longer than a month, but it does keep well up until then.

Can the ginger beer spoil?

If the ginger beer has been contaminated by mold, it is best to discard it. If the ginger beer has turned out flat, as long as it tastes good, then it is perfectly safe to drink. If the texture of the ginger beer is funny, i.e. slippery, but it still tastes good, it can still be consumed. We found these ginger beers are fine in smoothies and cooking, such as stir-fries.

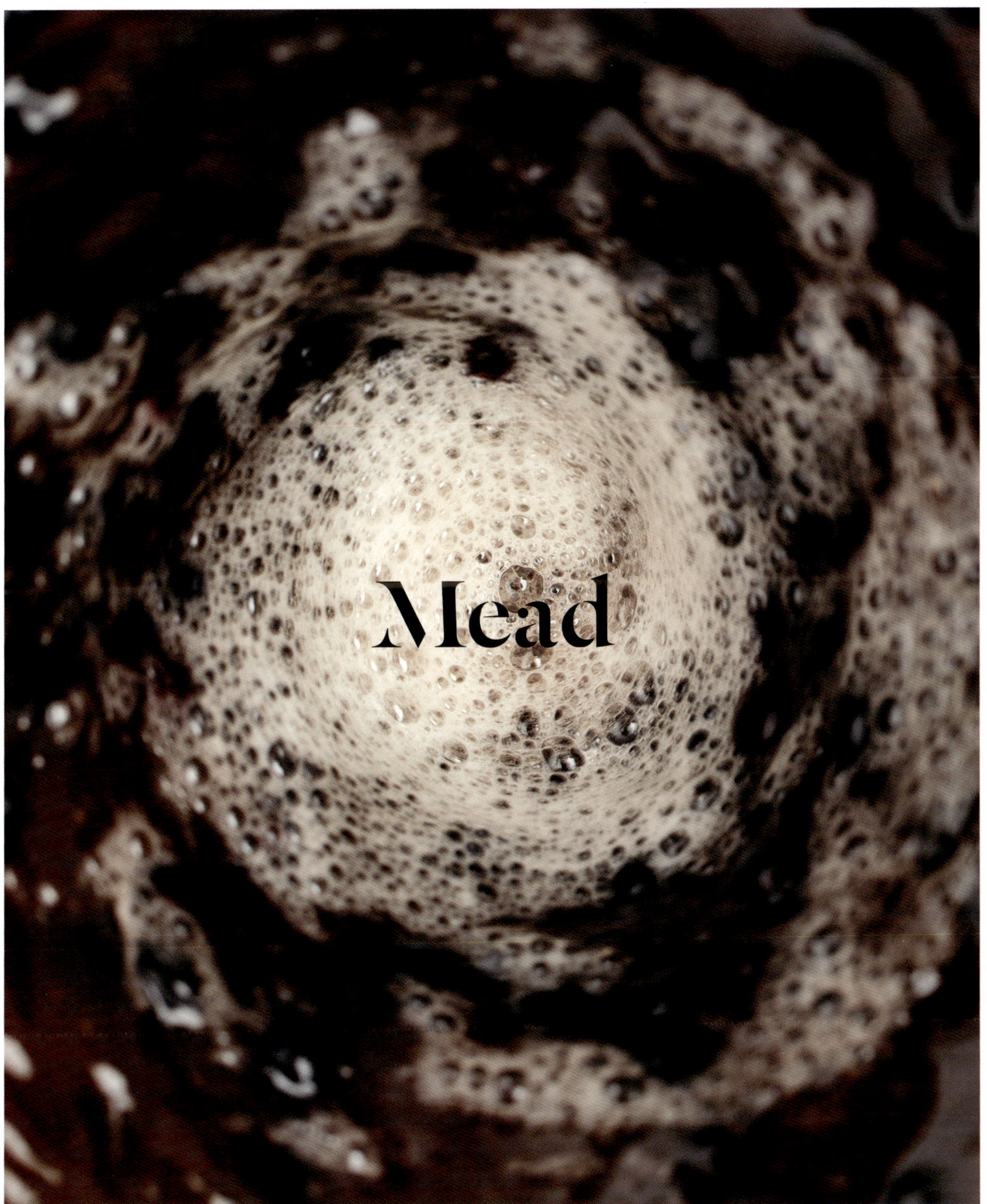

Mead

We love making and drinking honey mead. Honey mead or honey wine is a delicious alcoholic drink that can be enjoyed on its own, at room temperature, chilled in summer, mulled in winter, or mixed into cocktails. It is an easy, safe, and economical way to make alcoholic drinks at home. We make honey mead in different ratios of honey to water to produce meads in various strengths, which usually contain between 8 percent and 14 percent alcohol, and infuse the fermented liquid with fruits, herbs, and edible flowers to create unique and delicious drinks. This simple yet versatile technique has always been one of the main highlights of our fermentation workshops.

While we enjoy drinking mead, we don't drink alcohol regularly, making significantly more mead than we consume. We are easily tempted and inspired to make another batch when an ingredient that seems exciting becomes available in abundance or when the season of an ingredient we had used previously to make excellent mead returns. These days, we have about 40 liters (9 gallons) of mead in circulation, sitting in various demijohns and bottles for periods of three months to three years, which we mostly bring out for parties and to share with friends over a meal.

Mead is a celebration of local foods. Honey is made everywhere and easily accessible from your local beekeepers or online. Small beekeepers sometimes sell their honey in larger containers at a lower cost than purchasing honey from shops, which is a great way to source honey for mead making. We buy our honey in 4 liter (140 fl oz) batches at a time, from our local beekeepers, Mike and Sharon, who also care for the hives on our farm.

While most commercial honey mead is made using commercial Champagne or wine yeasts, we make mead using the natural yeasts found in the air and in the honey itself. Any type of honey will be suitable to make mead, and will add its own unique profile.

We have made hundreds of liters of honey mead in 4 liter (140 fl oz) demijohns. Every single batch came out wonderful and had not been contaminated by acetic bacteria. When we compare this success with the sugar-based wild fermented fruit wine we used to make, which had about an equal chance to become delicious wine or delicious vinegar, honey wines become even more attractive.

The simplicity, versatility, and dependability of honey wines made them one of the earliest alcoholic drinks enjoyed by humans. Honey, water, and time, what can be easier? Archaeobotanical analysis from samples of uncontaminated ancient liquid vessels shows that honey was used over 10,000 years ago. In his fascinating book *Ancient Brews*, Professor Patrick E. McGovern, an expert in the field of biomolecular archaeology, describes (and attempts to re-create) various ancient drinks, considered co-ferments, which combine mead, wine, and beer.* While we haven't played with co-ferments yet, we are looking forward to tasting our latest experimental batch, and infusing cacao nibs and chili into our honey mead, as used in Patrick's re-created drink, theobroma, the earliest recorded drink using cacao. As honey has antibacterial and antifungal properties, it will not spoil and will not ferment at high concentrations. Diluting the honey with water is what allows the fermentation; and the less water, the slower the fermentation.

There are many variations to honey meads, from infusing various ingredients to changing the honey-to-water ratio and the duration of the fermentation. These variations affect the sweetness/dryness of the drink, the flavor profile, the alcohol level, and even the texture. As honey mead is so versatile and simple to make, it is enjoyed around the world.

The alcohol content of the mead you make will be higher with less water, such as in the one-part to three-parts honey-to-water ratio in the Blueberry-Infused Honey Wine recipe on pages 138–40. Conversely, the alcohol content will be lower when more water is used to dilute the honey, as in the one-part to four-parts honey-to-water ratio in the Viola Flower-Infused Honey Wine recipe on pages 135–37. The honey-to-water ratio can even go down to one part to 10 parts, which is referred to as short mead and results in much quicker fermentation—it's ready within weeks—to become a completely different drink.

The sweetness of the mead is greatly influenced by the duration of the second fermentation; your mead will be sweeter with shorter fermentation periods, and semi-dry or dry with longer fermentation periods.

Other factors that will influence the flavor and time it takes for the mead to be ready include the type of flowers the honey was made from, the sugar and microorganism contents, water percentage, pH, additives used, and strain of dominant wild yeasts.

---

* Patrick E. McGovern, *Ancient Brews: Rediscovered and Re-Created*, first edition. New York: W.W. Norton & Company, 2017.

Raw, unpasteurized honey contains about 85 percent sugar (fructose, glucose, and sucrose), enzymes, amino acids, vitamins, minerals, organic acids, and phenolic compounds. Honey is not just sugar; everything in it affects the fermentation and taste of the honey mead.*

Equipment

Making honey mead at home requires only minimal equipment and financial investment. A demijohn, airlock, and syphon, which can often be sourced second-hand, are the only specialized pieces of equipment. Four-liter (140 fl oz) demijohns are widely available from brewing supply stores and online. Once you get the hang of making mead, you might want to make two demijohns with the same ingredients (perhaps with slight variations), as while 4 liters (140 fl oz) seems like a lot, it can run out quickly, so making double the mead in a 10 liter (2.25 gallon) bucket and then dividing it into two demijohns makes good sense.

For the primary fermentation, any stainless-steel pot or food-grade bucket will do fine. Don't use aluminium, enamel pots with exposed iron, or cast-iron pots.

For the secondary fermentation, a demijohn is preferred, but a bucket or jar with an airlock will also be suitable. You can use other vessels without an airlock and burp them regularly, but for the price, an airlock is very much worth the investment.

Any bottles that have a good air seal can be used to store your mead. We often reuse wine bottles, which we clean and then sanitize with boiling water. When making sparkling mead, you must use bottles that can handle the fermentation pressure that builds up in the bottles. We use the same flip-top bottles as we do for kombucha and ginger beer.

---

* Landis W. Doner, "The Sugars of Honey—A Review," *Journal of the Science of Food and Agriculture* 28, no. 5 (1977): 443–56, https://doi.org/10.1002/jsfa.2740280508.

Basic Mead

Making mead is a simple process.

Honey and water at a ratio of 1:3, 1:4 or 1:5

Mix the honey with the water in a food-grade container (bucket, pot, bowl) and cover it with a cloth such as a kitchen towel to prevent flies from accessing the fermented liquid. We refer to this stage as primary fermentation.

Stir the liquid once or twice a day until bubbles start to form. Once bubbles are formed, within 3 days to a week depending on the room temperature, transfer the liquid to a container that can exclude air from entering but release gases. This container can be a glass jug (demijohn) or jar with an airlock, or a fermenting crock. We refer to this stage as secondary fermentation.

Once the mead fermentation has slowed down, which can be easily observed when using an airlock as the bubble activity reduces, the mead can be enjoyed, bottled, or racked (see page 132). Depending on the honey-to-water ratio, the drink will be ready in months or years. Depending on how you like your mead, you can enjoy it when it is still sweet, semi-dry, or dry.

We often leave the mead in the demijohn until we need it to make a new batch or we run out of bottled mead. Once the fermentation has slowed down, usually within 6–8 weeks, the mead can be bottled.

Racking

While we rarely do so, racking your mead is another possible stage to add when making mead. Racking is the process of transferring the liquid from the secondary fermentation to another vessel under an airlock without the sediments—referred to as lees, which are dead yeasts and other particles—so that they won't affect the flavor of the mead. While it's a useful stage when aging the mead once the secondary fermentation has subsided, usually within 3–4 months, we admittedly didn't make many controlled trials to compare racked and unracked wines. We happily enjoy unracked wines and find the mead has excellent clarity and is not cloudy at drinking time. Professional mead makers prefer to rack their mead multiple times to eliminate all sediments.

Another use of racking is infusing other flavors into the mead or making Sparkling Mead (see page 146). When adding spices, for example, doing so after the second fermentation, in which gases are released from the liquid, will help retain the spices' full flavor. We did this when we added cacao nib to our theobroma-inspired honey wine (see page 128).

Infused mead

We often add fruits, herbs, and edible flowers to the primary fermentation. Each infuses flavors, nutritional value, and naturally occurring wild yeasts into the liquid that will turn into honey wine. By including these ingredients in our primary fermentation, we invite the wild yeasts they contain into the party to enjoy the diluted honey liquid and help create a unique, delicious drink. Another bonus of using fruits, herbs, and flowers in the primary fermentation is that it usually speeds up the fermentation and makes it more robust than honey and water alone.

If using additional ingredients, before transferring the liquid from the primary fermentation to the secondary fermentation container, sieve out any particles you used to infuse the liquid. Fermented fruits sieved from the liquid can be eaten and enjoyed as is. You can use the herbs and edible flowers mixed with water to make a delicate drink before discarding them into the compost.

As you experiment with the ingredients you have access to, you will learn what ingredients make the honey mead you enjoy the most. In the recipes on the following pages, we include ours.

Purple Peach
Cappings

Viola Meat
cappings Dec 2019
Persimmon Meat
June 2020
Chesthut Meat
March 2019 3:1

Viola Flower-Infused Honey Wine

Makes 4 liters (140 fl oz)

One of our favorite honey meads is infused with viola flowers, also known as pansies. You can use any variety of edible viola flowers, and there are many to choose from. We grow a mix of different colors and patterns of violas for their flowers throughout the spring, summer, and autumn as part of our approach to a healthy garden ecosystem. They are easy to grow, and when planted densely, create a mat of edible flowers. We have been supplying cafés and restaurants with these beauties we grow in our market garden. Occasionally, we harvest the whole patch and end up with a larger quantity of flowers than we need, which are too good to waste, and therefore call for another batch of viola honey mead.

The floral aromas of the viola flowers resonate very well with the honey's floral tones to create a truly magnificent drink. We prefer viola mead at a one-part to four-parts ratio of honey to water, but the higher one-part to three-part ratio is also delicious and goes great when added to cocktails. Another advantage of the one-part to four-parts ratio is that while it can be aged for years, it is usually a perfectly ready and enjoyable drink within 3–4 months. This is a big advantage if you need some homemade alcohol quicker than the 1–2 years it takes the one-part-honey-to-three-parts-water mead to be ready for drinking.

3.2 liters (112 fl oz) water
800 ml (28 fl oz) honey
100 ml to 2 liters (3½–70 fl oz) viola flowers

PRIMARY FERMENTATION

Add the water, honey, and edible flowers to a 6- to 10-liter (210 fl oz–2.25 gallon) food-grade bucket or pot. You can add as many edible flowers as you have available. Cover the container with a breathable fabric, such as a kitchen towel, that will prevent flies from getting in but will allow air in. Mix once or twice a day, preferably vigorously, to encourage air into the liquid and help the yeasts thrive.

SECONDARY FERMENTATION

Once the bubbles have formed on the surface, usually within 3–6 days, it is time to transfer the liquid to the demijohn. You have a bit of flexibility, and it doesn't need to happen ASAP,

(Continued overleaf)

but sooner rather than later is better, as you want to keep the liquid under an airlock to prevent acetic acid bacteria from coming in. This is the moment when, in our experience, honey outshines sugar. In sugar-based wild-fermented wines, the chance for spoilage at this step is huge, while with honey wines it is very low.

Pass the liquid through a cheesecloth or another tightly woven fabric that will filter out all the flowers. We often use a pot on top of which a sieve with cheesecloth can be placed securely. Once filtered, transfer the clear liquid to a demijohn.

Leave a gap of about 5 cm (2 in) of air at the top of the demijohn. As the liquid might froth, it is best to leave that gap to prevent liquid passing through the airlock, which can cause a bit of a mess and potentially push away the water that seals the airlock. If there is not enough liquid in the demijohn to fill it, and you are only short by a bit, just add water. If you are a cup or two short, it is best to mix the same honey-to-water ratio to fill in the gap.

Label the demijohn with the date you started the fermentation process, what's inside, and the honey-to-water ratio.

The fermentation time will mostly depend on the strength of the yeasts and the temperature. Expect bubbling to be frequent in the first few days and to subside over time. Usually, within 4–8 weeks you can transfer the mead into bottles or rack it into another demijohn or to a pot and then back to the same demijohn after it is cleaned.

We usually leave the mead in the demijohn without racking until we are ready to bottle, out of direct sunlight, anywhere from 3 months to 3 years.

BOTTLING

When bottling mead, it is best to use a siphon, a food-grade transparent short pipe, to help you transfer the mead without the sediments on the bottom. When doing this for the first time, having another person with you can be helpful.

The difference in height between the demijohn and the bottles enables the transfer of the mead. We find it best to place the bottles (or another demijohn if you are racking) in the sink and the demijohn on top of an upturned pot.

With clean hands, insert one end of the pipe into the demijohn and place it just above the sediment line. You can keep the syphon at the correct height above the sediment line by using a "racking cane" (also known as an "auto-siphon"), by getting a friend to hold it at the right height for you or by securing the siphon temporarily with tape. Take the other end of the pipe, and make a closed circle out of your thumb and index finger over it. Now for the exciting part: suck air through the finger circle you made, making sure to not have your mouth directly touching the pipe, as it can contaminate the brew. Now watch as the liquid transfers out of the demijohn, and place the end of the pipe inside one of the bottles or over a funnel that is set in a bottle. We usually use a funnel to fill the bottles with mead, as it gives us a bit more control, and it makes it easier to use our thumb as a cap to the pipe when transferring the funnel to the next bottle. Leave a small air gap of a few centimeters (inches) at the top of the bottles.

Another stage we consider a must—have a glass or two prepared to sample the mead, indicating the taste and how the fermentation progressed.

Remember to label the bottle with what's inside, the ratio of honey-to-water, the date you started making it, and, if you like, when it was bottled.

Serve at room temperature or chilled and enjoy with family or friends.

Note: If you don't have access to viola flowers or only have a few, you can use many other edible flowers, either as a single variety or a mix. Other edible flowers can include annuals, perennials, shrubs, and even fruit trees: cornflower, dahlia, rose, elderflower, borage, calendula, thyme, oregano, pineapple sage, evening primrose, hibiscus, feijoa, orange, lemon, peach, apple, or other flowers from fruits you might wish to thin.

Blueberry-Infused Honey Wine

Makes 4 liters (140 fl oz)

Honey mead is delicious when infused with fruits. The culinary term for honey, water, and fruit meads is melomel. Besides their wonderful flavor infusion into the mead, fruits are a great source of wild yeasts and will assist in primary fermentation. While any fruit you like will make a lovely honey wine, we especially love making it with blueberries. Blueberries keep their shape well during the primary fermentation, so make a funky little snack to enjoy after sieving, when the clear liquid goes into the demijohn.

While some volatile aromatic compounds will be released with the outgassing of carbon dioxide during the fermentation, we find that the fruits infuse heaps of flavor, and make wonderful mead. There are several different stages during which you can infuse fruit into the mead. We infuse fruits during the first fermentation, but the secondary fermentation stage is also common. If you want to try this option, you should add the fruit close to the end of the fermentation. Pay attention to the fact that the fermentation can resume, and the mead will start bubbling again. If this happens, allow bubbles to slow down significantly before bottling; otherwise, there will be too much pressure in the bottle, and it can explode.

Honey mead made with blueberries is terrific in any ratio, but we prefer to use the higher one-part to three-parts ratio. While it takes longer, usually between 1 and 3 years, the rich flavor is worth the wait.

3 liters (105 fl oz) water
1 liter (35 fl oz) honey
500 g–1 kg (1 lb 2 oz–2 lb 4 oz) fresh or frozen blueberries

PRIMARY FERMENTATION

Add the water, honey, and blueberries to a 6- to 10-liter (210 fl oz–2.25 gallon) food-grade bucket or pot. Cover the container with a breathable fabric that will prevent flies from getting in but will allow air in. Mix once or twice a day, preferably vigorously, to encourage air into the liquid and help the yeasts thrive.

SECONDARY FERMENTATION

Once the bubbles have formed on the surface, usually within 3–5 days, it is time to transfer the liquid to the demijohn. Pass the liquid with the blueberries through a sieve, or use a skimmer to remove them from the bucket.

(Continued on page 140)

Purple peach cuppings Sep 2022
Blueberry cuppings Sep 2022
Cuppings 1:4 Sep 2022
16 leaves 40g geranium rose

Leave a gap of about 5 cm (2 in) of air at the top of the demijohn. If there is not enough liquid in the demijohn to fill it, and you are only short by a bit, just add water. If you are a cup or two short, it is best to mix the same honey-to-water ratio to fill in the gap.

Label the demijohn with the date you started the fermentation process, what's inside, and the honey-to-water ratio.

The fermentation time will mostly depend on the strength of the yeasts and the temperature. Expect bubbling to be frequent in the first few days and to subside over time. Usually, within 4–8 weeks you can transfer the mead into bottles or rack into another demijohn or to a pot and then back to the same demijohn after it is cleaned.

We usually leave the mead in the demijohn without racking until we are ready to bottle, out of direct sunlight, anywhere from 3 months to 3 years.

BOTTLING

Follow the bottling instructions on pages 136–37. Age for a minimum of 1 year.

Serve at room temperature with or without ice and enjoy with family or friends.

Note: You can use any fruit, skin and all, you like and have available to replace the blueberries. Ideally, fresh, locally or homegrown, spray-free or organic. We make mead with figs, plums (Luisa plum is incredibly delicious), apricots, feijoas, persimmons, pears, grapes, strawberries, blackberries, elderberries, and peaches.

Cappings Honey Mead

Makes 4 liters (140 fl oz)

Another method we use to make honey mead is to use cappings honey. Cappings are a mixture of mainly wax and honey made by removing the caps of the beehive frames (honeycombs) to extract the honey from them.

Small beekeepers' operations can be an excellent source of cappings honey, or you can use your own if you have your own hives. Cappings are obtained when beekeepers unseal the wax cappings off the frames to harvest the honey. Many beekeepers prefer not to waste this beautiful resource and will collect the cappings throughout the season. Cappings can be fed back to the bees, and it often is. Beekeepers also keep it to make mead and extract the beeswax, which can be used to make candles, soaps, and ointments. See page 144 for how to make ointment using beeswax. Cappings honey makes for excellent mead, and in fact it is the primary source for our honey meads. While we do use pure honey to make mead, we first use any cappings we can get hold of, as we love the ethos of using a by-product to make something so wonderful as mead.

The process of making mead from pure honey and cappings honey is very similar and only differentiates at the primary fermentation stage.

There are two tricky bits to using cappings to make mead. One is to control the honey-to-water ratio, and the other is when it is time to extract the beeswax.

As the beekeepers extract the cappings honey from the honeycomb, the cappings contain a mixture of honey, wax, pollen, and often bee parts. The wax is mixed throughout the cappings honey, so it cannot be sold or used as regular honey. We are happy to let the primary fermentation include everything that ends up in the cappings for us to filter later. We don't find this negatively affects the taste.

3 liters (105 fl oz) water
1.1 liters (38½ fl oz) cappings honey
Fruit, herbs, or edible flowers (optional)

Add the water and cappings honey to a bucket or container and mix thoroughly. It will take a bit longer to stir this mix, which is ready when the honey is dissolved. If you wish to infuse fruit, herbs, or edible flowers, now is the time. Remember that they will likely be covered with wax when you strain them out and so will not be edible.

Mix once or twice a day, preferably vigorously, until bubbles are formed on the surface. Once the bubbling is sufficient, transfer the liquid through a cheesecloth or another tightly

4 Month old
cappings 1:4
with geranium
24g honey
28/1/23

woven fabric that will filter out all the beeswax and other particles, and into a demijohn. We often use a pot on top of which a sieve with cheesecloth can be placed securely. Once filtered, transfer the clear liquid to a demijohn.

From this point onward, the recipe is identical to using regular honey to make honey wine (see pages 130–37).

FIGURING OUT HOW MUCH HONEY YOUR CAPPINGS HONEY CONTAINS

The volume of everything contained in the sieve can be compared with the original amount of cappings honey you started with. For example, if you used 1 liter (35 fl oz) of cappings honey, and the material in the sieve (after being squashed to remove air) is 200 ml (7 fl oz), your cappings honey contains about 80 percent honey.

The cappings honey we use averages about 90 percent pure honey. While you can substitute pure honey with cappings without adapting the recipe, as the ratio of honey to water is very forgiving, you will get more consistent results, and the outcome you intended, by adding more cappings to compensate (as done in the recipe above).

It could be that the cappings you source will have a different percentage of honey, and we advise you to check by dissolving the honey and separating the remaining material out using a sample amount (i.e. 100 ml/3½ fl oz) to make sure you make the correct adjustment before you start your first fermentation.

EXTRACTING THE BEESWAX

Now that you have the wax in the cheesecloth, you can use several methods to heat it so the wax separates from the other particles.

Using a pot (our go-to method), place the cheesecloth with everything inside it, and ensure it is secure so it doesn't open. We tie ours with a string and weigh it down using a small plate that still allows the wax to float to the top of the pot. Fill the pot with water and heat up on low heat. The wax will melt and float as the water heats up, but everything else will be kept inside the cheesecloth at the bottom of the pot.

Remove from the heat and allow the wax to cool and harden. You will now be left with a lovely round piece of wax. Wash it under a running tap to clean it from residues that are sometimes found on the bottom side.

A solar dehydrator or an oven at low temperature will work well too. Use a tray at the bottom of the oven to collect the wax. Place a mesh on or above it, and place the cheesecloth on top of the mesh. Heat up the oven to 80°C (175°F), wait for the wax to melt into the tray, and turn off the heat once all the wax has melted. You will be left with a lovely piece of wax the size of your tray.

Easy Ointment from Beeswax Cappings

When we make mead out of cappings honey, we end up with quite a lot of beeswax. This wax is excellent for making ointments. While this isn't an edible recipe, we decided to include it here as a companion to our Cappings Honey Mead (see pages 141–43).

Making ointments at home is incredibly straightforward. At the most fundamental level, it is just mixing melted beeswax and oil; once cooled, you have an ointment.

From this starting point, an infinite variation is possible by using different oils, pre-infusing oils with herbs and other plant material, changing the ratio of wax to oil, and introducing textural ingredients.

Here is a recipe we enjoy making using calendula and lavender flower petals, two herbs we grow abundantly in our garden that are well regarded for their skin-healing properties.

INFUSED OIL

Calendula petals and lavender flowers
Olive oil, to top up

OINTMENT

40 ml (1¼ fl oz) beeswax (you can add more beeswax to make a stiff balm or lip balm)
200 ml (7 fl oz) infused oil

For the infused oil, fill up a 250 ml (9 fl oz) jar with calendula petals and lavender flowers. Ensure your flowers are not wet with dew, as a high water content can spoil the oil. Top up with olive oil until the flowers are fully covered. Leave the oil to infuse on the counter for a month. Strain the oil and keep it in a dark place or use it anytime.

Grate or shave the beeswax, removing any areas that captured sediments from the mead.

In a small pot over a low heat, heat up the infused oil, mix in the wax, and stir until the wax is fully dissolved.

Pour into small, clean, and dry containers and close with a lid. Once it has cooled down to room temperature, it is ready to be used as an ointment.

Sparkling Mead

Makes 4 liters (140 fl oz)

You can make sparkling mead from any mead very easily and quickly. To make sparkling mead, all that is required is to add a small amount of honey before bottling. Making sparkling mead requires bottles that can handle the pressure, such as you would use for kombucha or ginger beer. The pressure in the bottle will be too great for bottles not designed for carbonated drinks.

4 liters (140 fl oz) mead
48 g (1¾ oz) honey

Rack your mead, unless racked previously, into a container, such as a pot, bowl, or another demijohn (see page 132).

You can mix the additional honey in several ways. We found it easiest to prepare a honey-water mix by pouring a small amount of hot water into a jar along with the honey to dissolve it entirely. Add the dissolved honey water to your racked mead, mix thoroughly, and bottle.

Your sparkling mead will be ready in several days in warm weather, or can take up to 2 weeks in colder conditions.

Carefully open the lid (keep the opening away from your face) to check the carbonation after 3 days. If a robust carbonation is established, move your sparkling mead to the fridge. If not, leave for a few more days and check again. Once refrigerated for several weeks, it will be worth releasing some pressure to avoid too much pressure building up within the bottle, which can lead to it bursting in the fridge. The sparkling mead will store for many months in the fridge.

FLAVORING YOUR SPARKLING MEAD

Once your soon-to-be sparkling mead is bottled, you can experiment with additional flavors. This stage lends itself to spices, as they will keep well. We recommend opting for a mild flavoring, so only use a small amount. Spices you can play with include cardamom pods, cinnamon sticks, nutmeg, ginger, orange peel, licorice root, coffee, and cacao (powder and/or lightly-roasted nibs). Don't use fruits, as they can increase carbonation and pressure too much. You can use fresh or dried herbs, such as sage, geranium rose, rose petals, and basil, to name a few.

Trouble-shooting for Mead

The mead is too sweet and non-alcoholic

If the mead tastes sweet and non-alcoholic after months in the demijohn, this could be because the mead was placed in the demijohn too early, before the yeast had taken hold in the liquid during the primary fermentation. Another reason could be that the honey-to-water ratio is too high, and the high concentration of honey prohibits fermentation.

We once thought the wax component in our cappings honey was much higher and compensated with too much cappings. We ended up with a mead with a ratio of about 1:2.5, which, even after three years of fermentation, was still not ready and too sweet because the fermentation was too slow.

To fix this situation, you can pour the mead from the demijohn to repeat the primary fermentation. In the case of too much honey, add more water. To assist the fermentation, you can add fruit or other yeasty herbs and edible flowers.

Rosehip Elderberry Vinegar 2022
Peach Vinegar 2022
Apple cores Vinegar 2021

Vinegar

Vinegar is one of the oldest ferments made by humans. It has an incredible variety of uses in the kitchen, household and garden. In the kitchen, we use vinegar in salad dressings, marinades, pickles, stews, soups, sauces, dips, stir-fries, and as a splash over roasted vegetables. Vinegar adds unique flavors and sourness to our dishes. It is rich in nutrients and bioactive compounds that contribute to the prevention and treatment of disease.* Traditional medicines across the world prescribe vinegar for various ailments, and researchers are looking at its potential as a regularly consumed functional food.

Vinegar can be made from an enormous range of ingredients. Most cultures make and use vinegar from waste or excess from their most prevalent food ingredients and/or industries. Some varieties of vinegar include apple cider, wine, rice, malt, coconut, and, for us, peach.

To make vinegar, yeasts collaborate with bacteria. The yeast converts sugar into alcohol, and then the acetic acid bacteria convert the alcohol (ethanol) into vinegar (acetic acid). As the yeast and acetic acid bacteria are airborne, they are readily available to help us make vinegar.

The amount of sugar there is for the yeast to convert to alcohol affects the strength of the resulting vinegar. We make vinegar from ingredients we have in surplus as a way to preserve their flavor, and we are happy with whichever strength it comes to. We use sweeter fruits to produce more potent vinegar. So far, we haven't felt the need to supplement sugar beyond what was contained naturally in the fruits we use for our vinegar. Still, we keep this option in our tool belt.

When we want to use our vinegar for making pickles, which we often do, we choose one of our more potent brews. When necessary and if it's not easily determined by just the flavor, we'll use litmus paper to test the strength of our vinegar. We usually find our vinegar

---

* Nilgün H. Budak, et al., "Functional Properties of Vinegar," *Journal of Food Science* 79, no. 5 (2014): R757–64, https://doi.org/10.1111/1750-3841.12434.

is as strong as store-bought apple cider vinegar, at between 2 and 3.5 on the pH scale. We have made many batches of pickles over the years using our more potent batches of vinegar, with excellent results.

Another simple way to "make" vinegar, which we elaborate on in this chapter, is to have a "failed" attempt at making a fermented drink. Although we prefer to "make" these irregularly, our kitchen will usually stock some kombucha vinegar (left too long to ferment), wild-fermented-wine vinegar (got contaminated during the primary fermentation) or fermented honey mead (airlock water dried out and the air got in).

While we are happy to let our vinegar reach maturity on its own terms, there are two things we can do to speed up the process. We can increase the oxygen by frequent stirring, which invigorates the acetic acid bacteria. And we can inoculate the new batch by backslopping—pouring in a bit of mature vinegar or using a mother of vinegar—which will accelerate the process from several months to several weeks.

It is natural for a mother of vinegar to form in your homemade vinegar. This is a biofilm of acetic acid bacteria and yeast that develops in the vinegar and looks a lot like a kombucha SCOBY. Remove it prior to bottling. If you like, you can keep it alive in a jar with some vinegar until you are ready to use it in your next vinegar batch. A kombucha or jun SCOBY are good alternatives to a mother of vinegar.

Infusing Herbs

Infusing herbs in your ready-made home vinegar can be a great way to enhance its quality. Aromatic herbs such as sage, rosemary, thyme, oregano, mint, tarragon, lavender (more suited for a cleaning vinegar), bay leaves, basil, and dill can all impart some of their magnificence into the vinegar, which will carry through into whatever you use it in. Other ingredients to consider infusing include fresh ginger, chili, edible flowers, citrus peel, and whole (not ground) spices.

To infuse herbs in vinegar, take several sprigs of fresh herbs and place them in the jar or bottle of ready-made vinegar. It is best to add a generous amount so that their flavor will be substantial, not too weak. Taste after 2 weeks; if it is to your liking, that is enough time to let them infuse. If more flavor is required, leave it for up to 6 weeks. Take into account that after months pass, the herbal aroma will decrease. The fresh herbs' shape, texture and color will change over time and can spoil and contaminate your vinegar. After 2–6 weeks of infusing the herbs or ingredients, remove them from the jar or bottle. If necessary (and it often is), transfer the infused vinegar to another container using a sieve to capture any floating parts.

Storing Vinegar

Well-stored vinegar can keep for decades. Once your mature vinegar has reached peak flavor, store it in the pantry, away from sunlight, to prevent the flavor and color from changing over time.

While vinegar doesn't usually spoil, unpasteurized vinegar can over-oxidize. The best way to avoid vinegar over-oxidizing is to bottle it once it is ready into containers that allow minimal air exposure. Fill your bottles close to the rim to leave a minimal air gap. Tall wine bottles or thinner glass containers with tight lids are well suited for vinegar.

Over-oxidation happens when the bacteria in the vinegar run out of ethanol to consume. In the presence of oxygen, the bacteria will begin consuming the acetic acid, creating water and carbon dioxide. The reduction in acetic acid lowers the strength of the vinegar, which can ultimately create conditions for mold to ruin the vinegar. As you use your vinegar and the ratio of air to liquid changes, it is best to transfer the vinegar into a smaller vessel to preserve its quality.

We keep most of our vinegar in the pantry, leaving a couple of bottles on our kitchen bench. Keeping a selection of our favorite kinds of vinegar handy makes them accessible and encourages their use.

Fruit Vinegar

Making vinegar from fruits is one of our favorite kitchen homesteading activities, and it offers an exciting culinary experience. The process is simple, satisfying, and a great way to use an abundance of leftover fruit. Any fruit can be used to make this type of vinegar, and there is plenty of room to experiment as you can blend different fruits and later infuse them with herbs.

Any skin and fleshy part of the fruit can be used to make vinegar. We usually use peels, cores, and half-eaten fruit. At other times, when we make preserves or dehydrated fruits, anything that isn't at the quality of what we want but is not moldy gets to be made into vinegar. If we find ourselves with more fruit than we can eat or process, that too will go into making vinegar before it gets moldy.

Ingredients we make vinegar with include apple and pear cores and peels; part-eaten peaches and apples; over-ripe (but not moldy) plums, grapes, and strawberries; and over-ripe bananas or simply banana skins.

Making vinegar from fruits can be done at any scale with any quantity. We've made vinegar plenty of times in 1 liter (35 fl oz) jars when only small amounts of cores and peels were at hand and 2, 4, 10, and 20 liters (70 fl oz, 140 fl oz, 2.25 gallons, and 4.5 gallons) when a larger quantity was available. All quantities follow the same principles but require adjusting the container size to fit the fruit quantity you are after.

A wide food-grade container will help increase the surface area of our soon-to-be vinegar and give the acetic acid bacteria more oxygen, which will speed up the process. We often use food-grade buckets for larger batches and 1–4 liter (35–140 fl oz) jars for smaller ones. We cover the container with a muslin cloth, a thin fabric, or a kitchen towel, using a rubber band or string to secure it. We don't want any flies to join the vinegar-making party.

fruit (preferably homegrown or organic — non-organic fruits can have traces of fungicides)
water

Cut the fruit up into chunks. Place all the fruit pieces in a wide-mouth food-grade container or jar. You can place all the fruit at once, or as more fruit becomes available, add it over the coming week or two if there's enough room in your container to accommodate it.

(Continued overleaf)

Top up the container with water. Leave room at the top of the container to allow for easy mixing without the liquid overflowing. We usually end up with about half water and half fruit in our containers. Still, we opt for minimal water to cover the fruit when possible. It is better to have a more potent vinegar and dilute it later than the other way around. It is okay if some of the fruit is poking above the liquid, as with regular daily stirring, mold will not occur. Cover the container with a fine mesh or kitchen towel to keep flies out while allowing the mixture to breathe.

Over the first 2–3 weeks, stir the would-be vinegar with a clean spoon once a day (or every second day). Stirring prevents mold from taking hold and brings oxygen into the liquid, which helps speed up the process.

While there is no real need to taste your vinegar in the first days of making it, you can, especially if you want to enjoy your ferment at the alcohol stage. Caution: Delicious drinks may be found, and less vinegar might be made! A genuinely unique beverage we once enjoyed was a lovely rich, alcoholic banana drink made from a mix of banana skins and fruit. It never made it to the vinegar stage.

When the color of the liquid darkens, and most of the fruit's goodness is now in the water, it is time to strain the liquid through a fine sieve. Transfer the strained liquid back to a food-grade container and let it sit undisturbed for a couple of months with the fabric cover. After 2–3 months, the vinegar is ready to be used and, after removing the mother, should be transferred into bottles.

The kind of fruits used, their quality, their sugar levels, the air temperature, the consistency of mixing, and the length of time it was matured will give each batch of vinegar a distinct flavor profile. If the quality of one of your batches is questionable or perhaps a bit unpleasant (which can happen when using lower-quality ingredients, i.e. if they have mold or started rotting), you can use it for cleaning or in the garden.

Kombucha, Jun & Mead Vinegars

These delicious kinds of vinegar are too easy to make. In fact, we put a good effort into preventing our kombuchas, juns, and meads from turning into vinegar. When bottling time comes around, we customarily pour a small (or large) cup to taste our creation and understand how the fermentation has progressed. On the (rare, or so we try) occasion that a kombucha, jun, or mead tastes sour, we don't throw the drink away. Instead, we bottle it as vinegar or let it sit for another few weeks to get stronger, then bottle it as vinegar.

We treat these occasions as "happy accidents" and enjoy them for their unique flavors. However, kombucha and jun SCOBYs, which predominately contain yeast and acetic acid bacteria (AAB), can be deliberately used in the same way as a vinegar mother, not just to acidify teas but also to make juice, fruit, and any other type of vinegar.

In our household, we differ by our ability to enjoy kombucha and jun with varying degrees of acidity. In principle, the more you can enjoy them with higher acidity, the less sugar you consume. But even the staunchest among us can only handle so much.

If we have a SCOBY to spare, keeping one in the kombucha vinegar brew will help accelerate the process. If not, we don't stress about leaving the vinegar brew without a SCOBY. We suggest not leaving the SCOBY in the kombucha/jun vinegar for too long, as eventually it will run out of nutrients and starve.

In mead, vinegar can happen both at the primary fermentation and when aging in a demijohn. At the primary fermentation, if the brew has been contaminated with fruit flies or left for too long before racking, bacteria will start converting the alcohol into acetic acid. At the aging stage, if the water-filled airlock dries out, it will, unfortunately, allow bacteria in.

We particularly enjoy using kombucha, jun, and mead vinegar in salad dressings, soups, and marinades.

Apple
cores
Vinegar
2021
Rosehip
Elderberry
Vinegar
Peach Vinegar
2022
Mint
Jun
Vinegar
Pear
Vinegar
2022

Peanut Miso Vinegar Salad Dressing

Makes 400 ml (14 fl oz)

In 2010, we discovered the joy of a peanut butter tamari-based salad dressing. It is a delicious salad dressing that is a bit thick, which we enjoy on leafy salads, and occasionally on steamed vegetables on rice.

Over the years, as we've been enjoying more and more homemade miso it replaced the tamari we used to use, as reflected in the recipe below. With a slight modification to the recipe, you can substitute the miso with tamari or soy sauce and reduce the water or vinegar added.

When we want to show off and celebrate the signature fine leaf salad we grow and make in our market garden—"The Best Salad Ever"—we serve it with this salad dressing.

We tend to make this in the jar we will store and serve from. You can also make it in a bowl or a blender for a smoother texture.

50 ml (1¾ fl oz) vinegar
100 ml (3½ fl oz) water
50 ml (1¾ fl oz) aged miso
45 ml (1½ fl oz) honey
1 tablespoon toasted sesame oil
150 ml (5 fl oz) crunchy peanut butter

Start by pouring the vinegar and water into the measuring jar. The ratio of water to vinegar can change depending on the strength of the vinegar you are using. This recipe is perfect for using milder kinds of vinegar, which can substitute for some of the water.

Add the miso and honey to the jar and mix well. You can increase the honey content if you prefer a sweeter salad dressing.

Add the toasted sesame oil and peanut butter and mix well. This recipe is made with fresh peanut butter in mind. If your peanut butter is dry, add your choice of oil to compensate.

The viscosity should be thick but runny. At first the dressing might seem too thin, but over time the peanut butter will absorb the liquids, which will thicken the dressing. If this happens, add small amounts of water until the desired texture is achieved.

This salad dressing can be used straight away or stored for later use. It keeps for several weeks at room temperature and can be kept for months if stored in the refrigerator.

Mustard Seed Vinegar Salad Dressing

Makes 350 ml (12 fl oz)

Mustard vinaigrette was a staple in our homes growing up and was the go-to with a green salad. This is a delicious version we make on the farm for a salad dressing that is always a success. You can use yellow or brown mustard seeds. We use brown seeds, which are more pungent than the milder yellow variety.

This recipe has two stages. The primary one is to make the base dressing, which can be stored in the pantry or the fridge for months. And the second is adding lemon juice just before using it. Using the recipe this way gives the best of both worlds—creating a non-perishable delicious dressing base while still enjoying the added benefits of the fresh lemon flavor.

Besides enjoying this salad dressing on leafy green salads, it is well suited to be used as a marinade for fish and chicken and drizzled on grilled and steamed vegetables.

For a simpler version of this recipe, you can use already-made mustard, homemade or store-bought, instead of soaking the mustard seeds in vinegar and blending them.

100 g (3½ oz) mustard seeds
Water, to cover
150 ml (5 fl oz) vinegar
50 ml (1¾ fl oz) honey
5 g (⅛ oz) salt
1 teaspoon cracked pepper
150 ml (5 fl oz) extra virgin olive oil
Freshly squeezed lemon juice, to serve

In a bowl or jar, soak the mustard seeds in water. Leave them to sit for 12 hours or overnight. This process will assist in removing the phytic acid found in the seeds (see pages 164–65). Drain the mustard seeds.

In a blender or food processor, place the drained mustard seeds, vinegar, honey, salt, and pepper, and blend in pulses for about 1 minute. Add the olive oil and blend briefly, just until the olive oil has been evenly mixed in. Pour the content into several small jars, and keep them in the pantry or the fridge.

When ready to serve, for about every 50 ml (1¾ fl oz) of salad dressing you will be using, add the juice of half a small to medium lemon. If not consumed entirely on the day it was made, this is best kept in the fridge and used within a week.

Trouble-shooting for Vinegar

Mold developing on the top of the jar

Mold can be caused by infrequent stirring. If it is green mold, it is best to discard the contents into the compost pile. Make sure to stir your vinegar daily.

Sediments form at the base of the vinegar

Sometimes sediments will form in your vinegar. Sediments are not a health risk and are fine to consume. It is basically fruit particles suspended in the liquid that weren't sieved out and, over time, have settled at the base. You can rack the liquid by transferring your vinegar into another container, except for the bottom few centimeters, to help clarify it.

Vinegar Notes

Household and cleaning uses for vinegar

Vinegar is safe to handle, biodegradable, and unlikely to leave harmful residues on surfaces. It is a very versatile material and can be used to clean food surfaces, walls, floors, windows and ceilings; to reduce lime deposits in kettles, dishwashers, domestic pipes, and tanks; as a fabric softener for laundry; and even for hair washing.

When using vinegar for cleaning, a base of 50 percent water and 50 percent vinegar is a standard ratio. It is advisable to test a small patch of whatever you intend to clean with the solution first to make sure no harm is done before using it on a larger scale. This is especially important for carpets and sensitive fabrics.

Use of vinegar in animal care

Vinegar can occasionally be added to water for pets, poultry, and farm animals at a ratio of 0.5–2 percent. The vinegar will keep the water fresher, repelling bacteria and algae from the water containers.

Studies with chickens have shown that supplementing them with live unpasteurized vinegar helps them digest their food and absorb nutrients more effectively. [*,†]

---

* Sohail Hassan Khan and Javid Iqbal, "Recent Advances in the Role of Organic Acids in Poultry Nutrition," *Journal of Applied Animal Research* 44, no. 1 (January 2016): 359–69, https://doi.org/10.1080/09712119.2015.1079527.

† Parviz Allahdo, et al., "Effect of Probiotic and Vinegar on Growth Performance, Meat Yields, Immune Responses, and Small Intestine Morphology of Broiler Chickens," *Italian Journal of Animal Science* 17, no. 3 (3 July 2018): 675–85, https://doi.org/10.1080/1828051X.2018.1424570.

Sourdough & Fermented Grains

Our sourdough-baking journey started in 2007. We were staunch vegans at the time and baked sourdough bread twice a week in a small convection oven. Yotam especially enjoyed using leftover dishes and incorporating them into the dough, to bake a unique and flavorful bread while reducing kitchen waste.

As years pass, we have had many episodes of sourdough baking, each time gaining new insights, refining the practices, and enjoying keeping a new pet starter made from wild yeasts and bacteria. In recent years we have enjoyed making sourdough bread that bursts with flavor and has a great texture, lower acidity, and a crunchy crust.

At the start of 2023, Eviatar Karni, a professional baker, came to spend a couple of months with us on the farm. We wrote this chapter with his help and support, for which we are very grateful. Eviatar's depth of knowledge about sourdough and pro-baking skills revised the way we approached our baking, and fine-tuned our recipes.

Humans domesticated grains because these are generalist plants that are easy to grow and store the seeds of. Grains grow well in a variety of conditions, from flooded plains to disturbed tilled soils, and densely too. Over several millennia our relationship with the grain we grew changed: from foraging wild stands and growing grains as part of a mixed foraging, gathering, and cultivation diet and lifestyle, they became *the* staple for agrarian cultures in various times and places.[*]

Grains produce edible seeds, which need to protect their nutrients until they are ready to grow into new plants, and they do so by making and containing phytic acid. Phytic acid is a form of phosphorus present in grains, legumes, and nuts that is considered an "anti nutrient" because it binds nutrients including protein, starch and, most importantly, critical minerals such as zinc, calcium, iron and magnesium, limiting their bioavailability.[†] Before we carry on, we want to acknowledge that phytic acid has also been found to have a positive effect on several diseases such as colon cancer.[‡]

---

* James C. Scott, *Against the Grain: A Deep History of the Earliest States*, Yale Agrarian Studies Series (New Haven and London: Yale University Press, 2017).

† Ehsan Feizollahi, et al., "Review of the Beneficial and Anti-Nutritional Qualities of Phytic Acid, and Procedures for Removing It from Food Products," *Food Research International* (Ottawa, Ont.) 143 (May 2021): 110284, https://doi.org/10.1016/j.foodres.2021.110284.

‡ Feizollahi, et al.

While soaking grains and discarding the water can help reduce phytic acid, fermenting grains or flours, such as in sourdough, lowers the pH to an optimal level for the degradation of the acid. Sourdough can also introduce enzymes that break it down to non-harmful form.* This makes fermentation an important process in significantly increasing the nutrient value of bread and grain dishes.

While the reduction of phytic acid is reason enough to ferment grains, there is also the added flavor and texture. Fermenting grains adds richness and unique flavors and texture, making them not only more wholesome, but also tastier. Just like in other types of ferments, you can choose how and for how long to ferment your grains, and achieve the flavors that most suit your palate.

---

* Feizollahi, et al.

Starting & Maintaining a Sourdough Starter

Fermenting flour at home, whether with a fresh sourdough starter or one that has been passed down through generations, allows us to make our dough rise without the use of industrial yeasts. As the yeasts, lactic acid bacteria (LAB), and acetic acid bacteria (AAB) in our sourdough starter consume the starch in the grains, they release carbon dioxide, which gets trapped in the web of proteins (gluten, for example) and make it rise. How wonderful it is that hard grain seeds can turn into fluffy breads and pastries thanks to this culture of bacteria and yeast! Microbial activity also contributes flavors and textures to sourdough bakes and increases nutrient availability and shelf life.

Making a new starter is easy. All around us and in the flour we use, there are abundant and complex communities of both yeast and bacteria. When we make a new starter, we entice them with water and flour to feast on and colonize. This practice of inviting wild yeast and bacteria makes each starter community unique while performing the same function of rising dough.

At times, when we are in a hurry to make a new starter, we will kick-start the process by adding yeasts from other ferments, such as a ginger bug if we have it going (see page 119), or even by adding some unwashed organic fresh or dried fruit. Though this shortens the process, because the starter will then live on for a long while, over a few feedings the community will develop and stabilize, and the wild yeast and bacteria will join that symbiosis, so they are not excluded.

We used to start the process with 1 cup of flour and 1 cup of water. We now use a smaller amount, producing a stronger starter and creating less waste as our friend Eviatar recommended. We have adopted this technique to use only 30 g (1 oz) of flour and 30 ml (1 fl oz) of water to start the starter. The principle with this method is to always have more new flour and water compared with the overall starter in the jar. This is best achieved by keeping a small starter amount (about 15 g/½ oz) and then feeding with flour and water. The rest of the starter can be tipped out into the discard jar—see the discard section (page 169) for what to do with it.

Starter

"Starter" is our preferred term for "sourdough starter," which is the flour, water, and symbiotic microbe mixture that we feed regularly—our long-term companion to sourdough breadmaking. It has many synonyms such as "culture," "mother," and just "sourdough."

Sourdough Starter

FOR THE INITIAL STARTER
30 ml (1 fl oz) water
30 g (1 oz) wheat, spelt, or rye flour

FOR DAILY FEEDING
30 ml (1 fl oz) water per day
30 g (1 oz) flour per day

TO MAKE A SOURDOUGH STARTER

Place 30 ml (1 fl oz) water and 30 g (1 oz) flour in a jar, mix well, and cover with a cloth. Use a rubber band or whiteboard marker to mark the starting height of the mixture. Keep it in a warm place.

When feeding the next day, tip out 45 g (1½ oz) into your discard jar (see page 169), leaving about 15 g (½ oz) in the jar. Add to the jar the feeding amounts of water and flour, mix well, and cover with a cloth. This is known as a 1:2:2 (starter:flour:water).

Repeat this process every day for about a week, keeping 15 g (½ oz) and adding 30 ml (1 fl oz) water and 30 g (1 oz) flour daily, until the starter doubles in volume 8–12 hours after feeding. This is easy to see when using a rubber band or marker. If you occasionally miss a day of feeding, no major harm will be done, as the starter is robust and extremely hard to kill.

After 3–5 days, the starter will start to bubble. While it is ready to be used, the culture will keep evolving, become more complex, and generally stabilize after several repeated feedings. Once your starter is active, you can either use it for your leaven (see page 173) or give it another feed and keep it in the fridge until you are ready to start making your next sourdough bread (see Refrigerating your starter, opposite).

An indication of a starter that is ready to use in baking is that it is active and bubbling.

MAINTAINING YOUR STARTER

When you are ready to use your starter, or take your starter out of the fridge for the next bake, for most recipes you can use it straight to make a leaven (see page 174). Some recipes require an additional feed of 1:2:2 before using the starter to make a "young leaven."

Once you have made your leaven, taking a bit from it as your next bread starter is the best practice. Take 40 g (1½ oz), place it in a new jar, and move it to the fridge until you next bake. Another option is to use the jar that previously held the starter but is now empty except for the residual starter. This residual starter stuck to the jar is enough to facilitate inoculating new flour, so avoid rinsing it and add 30 g (1 oz) flour and 30 ml (1 fl oz) water.

If you notice that there is a liquid forming (known as hooch) at the top of your starter, it means that either your starter needs less water when being fed—follow up with only flour in the next feeding—or that it is hungry and that you should feed it more regularly.

Once we started treating our starter this way, avoiding having too much "old" starter in the jar and adding more flour and water, we enjoyed a much more active starter.

MAKING A FLOUR MIX FOR FEEDING YOUR STARTER

While you can use a single type of flour (white wheat, whole wheat, spelt or rye) to feed your starter, you can also make a mix of flour to feed it with. We often make up a jar with the following flour mix: 50 percent white wheat, 25 percent whole wheat, and 25 percent rye. This combination provides a wide range of nutrition to the starter and has the benefit of being a versatile starter that intimately knows all the main types of flour we like to use in our bread. If you change your starter-feeding flour, give it a few feedings to adjust to the new food before using it.

REFRIGERATING YOUR STARTER

Depending on your sourdough bread-making habits, and unless you bake most days of the week, it might be best to keep your starter in the fridge for the most part to avoid daily feeding, keep your starter at maximum health, and avoid creating large quantities of discard.

When you take out 40 g (1½ oz) starter from a newly mixed leaven, it can go straight into the fridge as it had been fed during the leaven-making process. If you are not using your starter weekly, you will benefit from "waking it up" a day earlier than you would with a recently fed starter to let it come back to full activity. While a starter can be kept in the fridge for a couple of months and revived, feed it at least once a week for best starter health and place it back in the fridge. Consider leaving your starter at a lower hydration rate, for example by using a 1:2:1 (starter:flour:water) or feeding it with flour without water. This will slow the fermentation, and give a better buffer for irregular feeding.

As mentioned, the starter is hard to kill, so that's not the main issue. What you need to be concerned about is keeping a healthy balance between the starter's microorganisms to prevent the microbial population from steering too far from one that will make great loaves of bread. To rejuvenate your starter, give it regular feeding, and even feed it for a third time on the same day.

DISCARD STARTER

If you end up with too much starter, often referred to as the "discard," don't throw it away. Instead, place it in a sealed jar in the fridge, where it will keep for a few months. You can use the discard when making pizza bases and flatbreads instead of a portion of flour and water, or see our favorite way of using it on page 210 (spoiler: it involves pancakes).

Sourdough Bread Basics

Many factors affect the creation of the humble sourdough bread, including the chosen fermentation process; air temperature and humidity; which varieties of flour are used; how the flour was milled; the freshness of the flour; the microbial community in the starter; kneading the dough; the salt content; and the length of fermentation.

There are many ways to bake sourdough bread, each with its advantages and challenges. The world of sourdough is full of subtleties, and as you keep baking you will fine-tune your senses and skill to create better and better loaves. Before we get into sourdough bread recipes, we want to discuss some basic concepts and terms we find very useful in baking bread.

Pre-baking temperature

Sourdough bread is a very temperature-dependent process and is highly influenced by it. Sourdough will ferment and rise at a wide range of temperatures. While it is not essential to be accurate to the degree, as sourdough has a relatively short fermentation process with several stages there will be a massive difference between baking at different temperatures. A change of one degree can significantly influence the time it takes for the starter or dough to ferment and proof. For example, fermenting at 22°C (72°F) can take significantly more time than at 24°C (75°F). Having a thermometer in the house or next to your sourdough bowl is handy for observing and learning how the dough ferments in your kitchen.

The recipes in this chapter are based on an average room temperature of 24–25°C (75–77°F). You can make some adjustments: if your average temperature is lower, use warm water to compensate; or use cold and even icy water when it is hotter. Most likely, the fermentation times will be different for you throughout the year as the temperatures change, and it is best to use the physical indicators of the bread rather than by adhering to timetables alone. Regularly monitor your dough, and move to the next stage only when it is ready. A good trick to check on your dough's progress is to use a whiteboard pen or a rubber band to mark on the container where the dough was when it started, making it easier to see its progress.

Flour

Use the freshest flours you can get access to. While we grow most of our own foods, so far we have not been growing grains for flour. We mostly purchase our flour directly from organic and local farmers who grow and mill it. Knowing where our grains come from, we are supporting locally grown, cover-cropping and, when possible, biological organic regenerative soil care practices.

It is often hard to identify the age of the flour at the shop, but it is worthwhile to access fresher flour that has not gone rancid. The germ, with the oils it contains, is what goes rancid first. However, fresh flour will have more variation in how it responds when making dough. Working with fresh flour, in combination with hydrating the dough and fine-tuning the amount of water, might result in slightly less predictable bread but an increased flavor and nutritional value. If you have access to a flour mill, you can purchase grains and mill them close to the baking time.

Leaven

We use the term "leaven" to describe the portion of dough (water, flour, and starter), which we make as a separate batch, to give us a robust and balanced yeast and bacteria community that will then feast on the rest of the dough and go into the oven. See overleaf for instructions on making leaven.

The primary function of the leaven is to create a significantly more active starter with a balanced yeast-to-bacteria community, which will help make the bread proof and rise fast to give it great texture and flavor.

Using a leaven instead of a straight starter and increasing the amount of leaven in our recipes made a massive difference in the results of our bread. It made for a much quicker and more robust fermentation, resulting in airier and less sour loaves.

A great tool in your bread-making box is to be able to choose whether to add more or less leaven to either slow down or accelerate the time it takes for the bread to be ready. Another useful technique is to choose at what stage of maturity to use the leaven. Unless mentioned otherwise, our recipes call for leaven at its peak height. For sweeter recipes, such as the Challah (see pages 202–5), use the leaven as soon as, or slightly before, it reaches the peak. For a sour taste, use the leaven on the other side of the peak—just before it starts to deflate.

When you want to let the dough ferment faster, for example during the day for evening baking or in colder temperatures, use a larger portion of leaven in the dough.

When you want to let the dough ferment slower, for example for an overnight proof for baking in the morning, use a smaller portion of leaven in the dough.

Basic Leaven

This recipe can be read as 1:2:2 (starter:flour:water)

80 ml (2½ fl oz) water
40 g (1½ oz) sourdough starter (see pages 168–69)
80 g (2¾ oz) flour

To a bowl or a jar, add the water and then the starter. Mix well. Add the flour and mix again. Take out 40 g (1½ oz) of the leaven to use as your next starter.

Cover with a lid or cloth, mark the height with a rubber band or marker, and let it rest in a warm place until the leaven has doubled in size.

The float test

A good indication that the leaven is ready is to gently pick up a small chunk of leaven (without deflating it), and place it in a container of water. If the leaven floats to the top, it is ready to be used to bulk proof the dough. If not, give it more time. While this method is imperfect, it will be reliable when using lighter, primarily white flour.

Baker's percentage

A convenient and foolproof way to look at how to calculate ingredients when baking is to use "baker's percentage." In baker's percentage, recipes are written as formulas that are percentage-based instead of weight-based.

Basically, in baker's percentage the weight of the flour is used as a point of reference for determining the percentages of the other ingredients. The flour is always 100 percent, and all the other ingredients are expressed as a percentage of that. So if a recipe calls for 500 g (1 lb 2 oz) flour and 300 g (10½ oz) water, the baker's percentage for water would be 60% (300/500 x 100).

Baker's percentage does not need to add up to 100 percent.

Baker's percentages are used for other ingredients too, like salt, sugar, and leaven. For example, if a recipe calls for 150 g (5½ oz) leaven and 600 g (1 lb 5 oz) flour, the baker's percentage for the starter would be 25% (150/600 x 100).

Here is an example of baker's percentage from the pita recipe (which you'll find on pages 198–201):

100% — 600 g (1 lb 5 oz) flour
25% — 150 g (5½ oz) leaven*
63% — 378 ml (13 fl oz) warm water
2% — 12 g (⅖ oz) salt

*Since the leaven is made of flour and water, and has 100% hydration (see below), the final hydration of the pita dough will be 67% (453 water/675 flour x 100).

Hydration

Hydration refers to the amount of water in the dough, which is usually represented as a percentage compared with the flour. 100 percent hydration refers to equal amounts of flour and water, for example a 200 g (7 oz) dough with 100 g (3½ oz) water and 100 g (3½ oz) flour. A general guideline for hydration percentages for bread is approximately 70%.

Autolysation

Autolysation is a process in which the flour hydrates and starts to develop gluten. Autolysation happens when we add water and mix it with the flour, which can include or exclude the starter. Letting the dough rest for any amount of time is beneficial, so a minimum of 15 minutes will help, but an hour will have the best effect and shorten the time and energy required to knead the dough.

Hydrating the flour and working the dough helps develop the strength and structure of the gluten in our bread as the dough ferments.

It is better and overall easier to start adding water in smaller amounts and working with a drier rather than a wet dough. This is especially true when working with new flours. If you are unsure whether to add more water, the best thing is to work the dough for a bit and then, if it feels dry, add a small amount—say 30 ml (1 fl oz) of water for a 800 g (1 lb 12 oz) dough mass—until you feel you have got a cohesive dough. The kneading or folding of the dough helps the flour absorb more water, creating stronger gluten bonds. As you make sourdough bread, you will find what times and rhythms work best for your lifestyle. One way we hasten or slow the fermentation process is by using water of different temperatures. When we want to slow down the process, we will use very cold water from the fridge. When we want to hasten the process, we will add warm water up to 40°C (105°F).

If you are using an electric dough mixer, it will inevitably heat up the dough, so to counter this effect use cold water.

Mixing and kneading

After the dough has autolysed, this is the time to knead your dough. Invest 5–10 minutes for best results when kneading, followed by optional "slap and folding" (see below).

Working your dough, such as kneading, or using slap-and-fold techniques, helps develop and strengthen it. The way you handle the dough can have a huge impact on the development and strength of the gluten structure, pushes the water further into the flour, and traps the gas produced by the microorganisms, causing the dough to rise and creating the light and airy texture that we all love in bread.

Slap and fold involves lifting the dough and throwing it down onto the working area with a bit of force, "slapping" it. When the dough is back on the surface, it is then folded back onto itself. Repeat the process by turning the dough 90 degrees and slapping it again against the work surface. It is best to keep folding and slapping with the direction of the dough in a way that supports it to almost roll. Use relatively straight fingers to help you make this work, and keep practicing, as it takes time to get used to handling dough this way.

Bulk fermentation

Bulk fermentation, or the first rise, refers to the stage after the kneaded dough is allowed to rise.

For this fermenting stage of the dough, any suitably sized bowl will do, but ideally use a thick-rimmed bowl, like glass, which will also allow you to see the level of rise; or ceramic, to keep the temperature stable. We usually use a bowl double the size of any intended bake, a matching glass lid from one of our cooking pots, or a cotton kitchen towel so the dough doesn't dry out.

Determining when the dough has completed the bulk fermentation can be tricky. To avoid under- or over-proofing the dough, some of the best indicators are:

- The dough has nearly doubled in size and is full of gas.
- The taste (yes, the taste) of the dough is a pleasant yeasty and a bit tangy flavor (yes, taste it).
- Bubbles have formed at the bottom and sides of the bowl. You can see this if using a clear bowl, or when picking it up gently.

Folding

Once your dough is fully mixed, the fermentation kicks in. Forty minutes into the bulk fermentation, when the dough has relaxed, it is time to fold the dough, to organize the gluten structures. Folding will happen ideally three times during this stage of bulk fermentation—every 40 minutes for the next two hours, or at least once.

There are many different techniques to strengthen the dough and perform this task. One of them, the stretch and fold technique, involves stretching the dough out and then folding it over to the center, and repeating from each of four directions: left, right, top (aka north), and bottom (aka south). The process further develops the gluten structure. Stretch and fold helps achieve a more even crumb structure and prevent the dough from spreading out too much during the fermentation process.

Shaping your dough

When we first started making bread, we thought that shaping was just about getting the shape right. How mistaken were we. Shaping correctly makes a big difference to how well the bread will come out.

Before the final proofing stage, when you will let your dough rise for the last time before going into the oven, it is time to shape the dough. You should shape your dough in a way that encourages your bread to rise by creating surface tension. Creating a surface tension is

relevant for every baking method, even when the dough is placed inside a tin.

To make shaping easier, start by lightly dusting your work surface, your hands, and the top of the dough.

The most simple shape is a roundish ball, also referred to as a boule, which just means ball in French. To shape into a ball with maximum surface tension, position the dough so the smoothest side is on the top, and evenly tuck the sides under so they are slightly placed at the bottom of the loaf, and cause the dough to stretch. The result is that the ball is tighter than if it were just formed into a circle and placed on the tray.

The next most common shape we like using is an oval, or bâtard (meaning bastard, supposedly because it is a cross between a boule and a baguette). Take your dough and lay it on your workbench so it is a rough rectangle rather than a circle. Take one of the long sides and fold it over, about two-thirds into the other side. Take the other side and fold it on top, all the way to the other side. You are now left with a rectangle again. Take the top narrow side and fold it to the middle, then keep rolling and stretching the dough until all the dough is part of a tight log. Tuck in the ends and carefully place the dough on a tray with the seam side down, or in an elongated proofing basket with the seam side up—pinch to seal the seams before moving to the next stage.

Proofing

The next stage after shaping your dough is to let it proof. Proofing is the last rise before the shaped dough goes into the oven, and it can be done at room temperature or inside the fridge. A term for proofing in the fridge is "cold retard," because it retards—meaning delays, holds back, or slows down—the dough from continuing to rise as the yeast goes dormant.

During the proofing stage, the bacteria in the dough continue to work and ferment, breaking down the complex sugars in the flour, and releasing organic acids that contribute to the bread's flavor. This can be done at room temperature, which is a good option for bulk fermentation, proofing, and baking on the same day.

Proofing at cold temperatures is a great tool in the breadmaking toolkit, and an excellent strategy to use when you need extra flexibility. The dough can be kept proofing in the fridge for anything from several hours up to 24 hours. When you have time constraints, you might choose to combine cold- and room-temperature proofing by starting the process either in the fridge or on the bench, and ending it the other way around. When keeping the dough in the fridge to proof for a more extended period, pay attention that it doesn't overproof and lose its spring, which can happen when the bacteria runs out of food and will result in a flat bread.

Proofing can be done on a tray, inside a tin mold, and in a proofing basket. When proofing in the fridge, cover the dough with a lid, towel, or a bag to prevent the dough from drying out, which will affect its oven spring (see page 184).

Proofing baskets, also known as bannetons, are vessels that the bread can rest and ferment in and take the shape of before going into the oven. There are many shapes to choose from. For easier cleaning, it is best to use a liner, such as a lint-free tight woven kitchen towel or the fabric liner that came with the basket. When using a liner, dust it with flour to prevent the moist bread from getting stuck to it. While most bread proofing baskets are made from cane, you can use any bowl that you have in the kitchen in the same way.

Poking the dough

A good indicator for testing if the dough is ready to go into the oven is to poke it with your finger and see what happens. While you can never know, one of the following will likely occur:

- The dough immediately bounces back, filling the indent, indicating that the dough is under-proofed and needs more time.
- The dough bounces back within 2–3 seconds, filling the indent but often not entirely — perfect, your loaf is ready to be baked.
- The dough does not bounce back — the dough is over-proofed. Use it anyway, but avoid scoring (see below) and expect a flatter bread. Next time try to catch your dough earlier. You can also reshape it for flatbread or pizza bases, or place it in a tin to help it keep a good shape in the oven if that seems feasible.

Scoring

Scoring refers to cutting into the dough before baking to allow it to expand fully and rise in the oven, directing its shape and preventing it from cracking. The area of the loaf being scored is where the gases can push through and rise, as it is now the weakest area on the surface of the bread.

Using a very sharp blade makes a significant difference in scoring results. The cut doesn't need to be too deep; 5–10 mm (¼–½ in) is all it takes. Try different angles, such as a 30 percent cut rather than perpendicular to the loaf. Professional bread makers usually use a razor blade, often with a tool to hold it called a lame. At home, you can use any very sharp tool at your disposal, such as a craft knife or sharpened kitchen knife. You can wet or lightly oil the blade, which will reduce friction and help to create a continuous single cut. Avoid pushing down as you are cutting. When scoring, less is more.

If your knife is sharp and your bread is correctly proofed, you should be able to make cuts without a problem at room temperature, though it is easier to score when the loaf is cold. If the dough is over-proofed it will not score well, and it is best to avoid scoring it so it keeps the gases trapped in it.

Once the loaf is scored, it will start to deflate. So score just before the bread goes into the oven.

Baking, oven temperatures, and humidity

Always preheat the oven for baking bread. When the bread gets into a very hot oven, it will rise well and have a beautiful oven spring.

Unless otherwise stated in the recipe, turn the oven to 240–250°C (475–500°F), and let it get to temperature. If you use a Dutch oven (see page 184), place it in the oven to preheat before turning the oven on. Place the bread in the bottom third of the oven and close the oven door as quickly as possible to avoid losing heat. A way to keep the heat in the oven is to use a baking stone, which, due to its mass, will keep to the temperature of the oven before the door was opened and will immediately transfer that heat to the dough.

Another factor when baking in an oven is the humidity level. A well-made dough that has been scored will have the flexibility to allow the surface area of the bread to expand without rupturing. The term for this process of quick expansion in the first part of the baking is referred to as "oven spring" (see page 184). Having a high humidity in the oven at the time when the bread is substantially increasing in size will help it reach its full potential. Once the expansion stage ends, as the crust becomes rigid, it is best to reduce the humidity to allow the crust to form fully and crisp in a dry oven. At this point reduce the temperature to 220°C (425°F), and leave it on this heat for the rest of the baking time.

A bread that is not proofed well, or had a tough hard crust forming on the dough before baking, or was placed in a dry oven will likely be flat, dense, and moist or, as the term goes, a brick.

There are several options to facilitate adequate humidity levels for the first part of the baking: using a Dutch oven (see page 184), using a bread tin with a lid, using an oven with a steam function, or placing a heatproof tray, baking pan, or bowl at the bottom of the oven with hot water (and removing it around the middle of the bake).

You can bake any amount of loaves together that fit your oven, or if you are using a Dutch oven, it doesn't take much more energy to bake that second loaf. Go bread go.

Oven spring

Oven spring is when the dough rapidly expands in the first baking stage, usually about 10 to 20 percent in size during the bake's first 10–20 minutes.

Many factors influence how well the bread will rise in the oven: using a higher-protein white flour variety; using an active starter; autolysation; a full and correct proof (not over or under); kneading and working the dough; creating surface tension when shaping the dough; scoring; humidity in the oven; and baking in a hot oven from the get-go.

Dutch oven

A cast-iron pot with a tight-fitting lid, known as a Dutch oven, is increasingly popular among home breadmakers. A simple alternative is to use a casserole dish or a couple of cast iron pans placed on top of each other. Using a Dutch oven provides the humid environment needed for the bread to rise better and produce a more even crust.

Preheat the Dutch oven for at least 30 minutes, so place it inside the oven when you turn it on. Once your dough is ready and the Dutch oven is preheated, carefully place the dough in it and put the lid on. The lid helps trap the steam created by the bread, which helps your bread to rise and form a delicious crust. After two-thirds of the baking time has passed, remove the lid using heavy-duty oven gloves or two to three layers of towels. When placing the dough in the (hot!) Dutch oven, you can use parchment paper to help lower the dough (like a sling) or, if the dimensions suit, a small pizza peel.

Cooling and storage

After removing the bread from the oven, place it on a rack to let it cool evenly from all sides and for the crust to harden. We use a simple metal rack that we got at a second-hand store. Once the loaf has cooled down for a couple of hours it is ready to eat and will store well for 3–5 days inside an airtight container at room temperature. You can keep the airtight container in the pantry or a cool location in the house, and expect it to give you another day or two of shelf life.

When freezing the bread, cut it into slices and place it in an airtight container. While it is perfect for toast, you can use it for a sandwich as well.

Baking schedules

Here are two examples of the whole process starting from the moment the starter is out of the fridge. This is an approximate timetable; remember to check each stage for the indicators before moving to the next stage.

SCHEDULE #1

This chart follows the process of breadmaking described earlier, which includes autolysation, kneading, and folding.

Day and time	Action	Comments
Friday 8 pm	Making the leaven — feed straight from the fridge starter.	Remember to take out 40 g (1½ oz) as your next starter.
Saturday 7 am	Autolyse	
Saturday 8 am	Mixing — add the leaven and salt. Knead, or fold and stretch, or slap and fold, for 5–10 minutes. Return to the bowl.	Proceed with this stage when the leaven has doubled in size, and has a fresh (not sour) yogurt taste. At first it will look like the dough is going to break apart, but it will come together as you keep kneading or folding.
Saturday 8:15 am	Start of bulk fermentation	
Saturday 9 am, 9:40 am, 10:20 am	Folding	Fold at even intervals, at least once, or ideally three times (every 40 minutes).
Saturday 10:20 am	Bulk fermentation continues	No kneading or folding at this stage. Let this process go for another 2–2.5 hours.
Saturday 12:30 pm	Shaping the loaf and proofing	Proof at room temperature, unless preferring to bake the next day, in which case move to the fridge.
Saturday 5 pm	Scoring and baking. Preheat the oven to 240°C (475°F) — the highest setting. If using a Dutch oven, when the lid is off reduce to 220°C (425°F). Bake for 30 minutes with the lid, 15 minutes without.	Poke test (before baking) — touch the dough and look for it to bounce back slowly in 2–3 seconds.
Saturday 5:45 pm	Out of the oven — take the bread out of the oven once the crust has colored to your satisfaction and place on a rack.	As the loaf continues cooking outside of the oven, let it keep cooling to room temperature, for 2 hours if you can manage it.

SCHEDULE #2

This chart follows a no-knead breadmaking process. When making no-knead bread, skip the autolyse stage, as well as the kneading and folding. We make a lot of no-knead bread, and while it is not as airy as kneaded bread, it is still delicious.

Day and time	Action	Comments
Friday 8 pm	Making the leaven — feed straight from the fridge starter.	Remember to take out 40 g (1½ oz) as your next starter.
Saturday 8 am	Mixing — add the leaven and salt. Mix until everything is cohesive. Return to the bowl.	Proceed with this stage when the leaven has doubled in size, and has a fresh (not sour) yogurt taste.
Saturday 8:10 am	Bulk fermentation	Let this process go for 4–5 hours.
Saturday 12:30 pm	Shaping the loaf and proofing	Proof at room temperature, unless preferring to bake the next day, in which case move to the fridge.
Saturday 5 pm	Scoring and baking. Preheat the oven to 240°C (475°F) — the highest setting. If using a Dutch oven, when the lid is off reduce to 220°C (425°F). Bake for 30 minutes with the lid, 15 minutes without.	Poke test (before baking)— touch the dough and look for it to bounce back slowly in 2–3 seconds.
Saturday 5:45 pm	Out of the oven — take the bread out of the oven once the crust has colored to your satisfaction, place on a rack.	As the loaf continues cooking outside the oven, let it keep cooling to room temperature, for 2 hours if you can manage it.

Sourdough Bread

Makes 2 loaves

This base recipe includes general and specific instructions about how to bake a sourdough loaf, based on the terms we have described on pages 174–85 and following schedule #1 (see page 185).

You can change the types of flour and ratios in this recipe. When starting out with breadmaking, we suggest using at least half of the total flour amount as white flour, to better support gluten formation. Depending on the flours you use and the relative humidity, you might need to add more or reduce the amount of water you use to make the dough. The dough might seem wet at first, but don't make any changes until you finish the kneading or folding.

Like gardening, it takes time to learn the subtleties of breadmaking so you get the results you aim for; trial and error and keen observation are instrumental. Enjoy the process as well as the bread you will be making.

20% — 160 g (5½ oz) leaven
100% — 800 g (1 lb 12 oz) flour (60% white wheat, 20% whole wheat, 20% spelt)
67.5% — 540 ml (18½ fl oz) warm water
2% — 16 g (½ oz) salt

TOTAL FLOUR CALCULATION

800 (dough) + 80 (leaven) = 880 g (1 lb 15 oz)

TOTAL HYDRATION CALCULATION

540 (dough) + 80 (leaven) = 620 ml (21½ fl oz)
620 (total water) / 880 (total flour) x 100 = 70% (hydration)

MAKING THE LEAVEN

Make the leaven in a 1:2:2 ratio—40 g (1½ oz) starter, 80 g (2¾ oz) flour, 80 ml (2½ fl oz) warm water. Cover with a loose lid or cloth, mark the height with a rubber band or marker, and let it rest in a warm place until the leaven has doubled in size, over 8–12 hours.

Take out 40 g (1½ oz) of the leaven to use as your next starter.

AUTOLYSE

To a bowl, add 800 g (1 lb 12 oz) flour and 540 ml (18½ fl oz) water, and mix. Cover with a cloth or lid. Let the dough autolyse for 1 hour.

(Continued overleaf)

MIXING

Once the leaven has doubled in size, mix the leaven and the salt into the autolysed dough inside the bowl. When it becomes a cohesive dough, work the dough on the surface using your preferred kneading or folding technique (see pages 177–78) for 5–10 minutes.

The consistency of the dough after kneading or folding should be firm and not watery. Place the dough in a lightly oiled bowl, cover and set it in a warm place to start the fermentation.

BULK FERMENTATION

The bulk fermentation starts when the leaven has been mixed into the dough. During bulk fermentation, the dough will double in size. This could take 3–6 hours, depending on the room temperature and the strength of your starter.

FOLDING

Folding happens during bulk fermentation. Fold the dough one to three times over the next 2 hours.

SHAPING THE LOAF AND PROOFING

When the dough has risen, divide the dough in two and shape each half into a loaf (see pages 178–80) with a tight surface area while avoiding unnecessary deflating of the dough. Place on a lightly oiled tray, a floured proofing basket, or a loaf pan.

SCORING AND BAKING

While the bread is close to finishing proofing, preheat the oven to 240°C (475°F). If you are using a Dutch oven, place it in the oven before turning the oven on.

Poke the bread to check that it is proofed (see page 181).

Score your bread and place it in the warm oven. Follow the baking instructions on page 182.

OUT OF THE OVEN

Baking should take 45 minutes. Take the bread out of the oven once the crust has colored to your satisfaction; give it another 5 minutes if you want the crust to be darker. Let the bread cool down, on a rack, for 2 hours or more. Enjoy it on the day or store it (see page 184).

Sourdough Bread with Leftover Grains (No-Knead)

Makes 1 loaf

This is an adaptation of a quirky method of making bread with leftover dishes that we learned from Sandor Ellix Katz's book *Wild Fermentation.*

When you are in the breadmaking mood and you have a grain or legume dish that is still very much edible, but you have had enough of eating it as is, you can upgrade it, and your next loaf, by adding it to your dough. We've used rice here, but you can use other cooked grains too.

20% — 80 g (2¾ oz) leaven
100% — 400 g (14 oz) flour (80% white wheat, 20% spelt)
30% — 120 g (4¼ oz) cooked rice
63% — 250 ml (9 fl oz) warm water
1.8% — 7.5 g (3/16 oz) salt

Make the leaven with a 1:2:2 ratio—24 g (⅘ oz) starter, 48 g (1¾ oz) flour, 48 ml (1¾ fl oz) water. Wait until it doubles in volume. Take out 40 g (1½ oz) to use as your next starter.

Add the flour, rice, water, and salt. Mix until you have a cohesive dough. Place in a lightly oiled bowl. Bulk ferment, with no folding. Shape the loaf (see pages 178–80) and proof it in a bread tin. There is no need for scoring, but you can if you like.

Preheat the oven to 240°C (475°F). Bake for 30 minutes with a lid over the tin or steam. Remove the lid and reduce the oven temperature to 220°C (425°F). Bake for another 15 minutes.

Take the bread out of the oven once the crust has colored to your satisfaction. Place on a rack to cool for 2 hours.

Sourdough Pizza Base

Makes 5 medium or 3 large pizza bases

We love a good pizza party! We light our earth-built pizza oven a couple of hours ahead and gather friends and family around the table. Together we harvest and cut vegetables and herbs, grate the cheese, and organize all the other toppings. When the time comes, each person makes a pizza with their choice of ingredients and styles it as they see fit. As the pizzas fly out of the oven, we share them with each other, so everyone gets a taste. For the best homemade pizza we like to make a sourdough pizza base and use a homemade pizza sauce.

Some of our favorite toppings include garlic, fresh tomatoes, Dried Tomatoes in Olive Oil (see page 334), arugula, jalapeño, Pickled Olives (see pages 85–86), spinach, radish pod Misozuke (see page 246), oregano, basil, thyme, caramelized onion, leeks, Air-dried Cured Meat (see pages 298–301), microgreens, zucchini ribbons, walnuts, black pepper, and . . . pineapple.

35% — 175 g (6 oz) leaven
100% — 500 g (1 lb 2 oz) flour (80% white wheat, 20% spelt)
63% — 315 ml (10¾ fl oz) warm water
2.5% — 12.5 g (½ oz) salt
Flour or semolina for dusting the pizza dough
Homemade Pizza Sauce (see page 269)
Your choice of toppings
Cheese or vegan cheese

MAKE THE LEAVEN

Make the leaven with a 1:2:2 ratio—40 g (1½ oz) starter, 80 g (2¾ oz) flour, 80 ml (2½ fl oz) warm water. Cover with a loose lid or cloth, mark the height with a rubber band or marker, and let it rest in a warm place until the leaven has doubled in size, over 8–12 hours. Take out 25 g (1 oz) to use as the next starter. Feed it 1:1:1 to build back up to quantity.

MIXING

Mix together the flour, water, leaven, and salt. When the mixture becomes a cohesive dough, work the dough on the surface while kneading for 5–10 minutes (see page 177). Place in a lightly oiled bowl.

(Continued overleaf)

BULK FERMENTATION

Let the dough rise for about 3–5 hours, with no folding. The dough should roughly increase by 50%, not doubled as for other bread recipes.

SHAPING

Shaping for pizza starts by dividing the dough into the number of bases you would like to use. We use 200 g (7 oz) for a medium-sized pizza, but you can also make about 330 g (11½ oz) bases for larger ones. Each piece is shaped into a ball with a tight surface area (like a small boule), and placed inside a lightly floured tray or box with a cover.

PROOFING

Proof the dough at room temperature. If baking on the same day, the balls will be ready in 4–6 hours. If you will be baking the next day, let the dough balls proof for 2 hours at room temperature, and then transfer to the fridge. An hour before use, take the container with the dough out to thaw at room temperature so that it can relax.

MAKING THE BASES

Poke the dough to make sure it is proofed (see page 181). The balls should have increased in size and not feel tensioned. They are best picked up with a dough scraper.

Open the round dough balls into flat pizza bases in the shape and size you prefer. Dust your dough liberally, using semolina or flour, pushing the air from the center of the ball to the sides with your hands, creating a small rim on the perimeter, which will form a lovely crust when baked. For a thinner crust, you can use a rolling pin.

SAUCE AND TOPPINGS

Spread the pizza base with pizza sauce. You can pre-bake your bases after adding the sauce, for 2 minutes in a hot oven. This is useful if your base is thickish, so it can properly bake without burning your toppings.

Add your favorite toppings and cheese.

IN AN ELECTRIC OVEN

Preheat the oven to 250°C (500°F) and keep it at this temperature while baking. If you have a baking stone, this is a great time to use it.

Place the pizza in the top half of your oven and bake until crisp. Remove, then add any additional toppings such as greens or cured meat if you like. Enjoy while still warm.

(Continued overleaf)

FOR WOOD-FIRED PIZZA

Light the fire about 2–2.5 hours before baking. Start a small fire in the middle of the oven and let it heat up gradually. As the oven heats, keep increasing the heat by adding more wood to the fire. About half an hour before baking the pizzas, stoke the fire for the last time, using denser wood if you have any available.

Push the coals into a heap at the back of the oven a few minutes before baking, slightly hugging the sides. Blow on the bottom to clear it of ash and small coals.

The fire bricks at the bottom will be scorching, as the oven can reach temperatures of 300–450°C (570–840°F). You can use a peel to get the pizzas into the oven straight on the hot stones, or a pizza tray, which doesn't require a peel (we use a weeding hoe with a short handle). We place two pizzas next to each over and turn them regularly. The first pizzas will bake in a matter of minutes, so keep turning them regularly and take them out of the oven when crisp on all sides.

After about 30 minutes, shuffle the coals to move the ash aside and place them again at the back of the oven. The heat should be sufficient to bake for about 45 minutes, but if you want to bake pizza for longer, add wood to the coals at the back.

Once the pizzas are all done, use the oven to keep baking, with or without a door. We often line up bread loaves, sweet baked desserts, baked potatoes and kūmara (sweet potatoes), and a large meat roast with vegetables. Pay attention so that nothing burns, as the heat can be intense for a while.

Sourdough Pita

Makes 12 pitas

Pita, a flatbread with a handy pocket, is a staple food in the Middle East, and is enjoyed with a wide range of foods. This recipe is for small- to medium-sized, 13–15 cm (5–6 in) diameter, pitas. These are handy-sized pitas to fill up and enjoy as one piece or cut into two. We suggest making this recipe in a pan and enjoying your soft and delicious pita with any of your favorite dips, or try it with Sabich (see pages 58–59).

25% — 150 g (5½ oz) leaven
63% — 378 ml (13 fl oz) warm water
100% — 600 g (1 lb 5 oz) flour
2% — 12 g (⅖ oz) salt

Make the leaven in a 1:2:2 ratio—40 g (1½ oz) starter, 80 g (2¾ oz) flour, 80 ml (2½ fl oz) warm water. Cover with a loose lid or cloth, mark the height with a rubber band or marker and let it rest in a warm place until the leaven has doubled in size, over 8–12 hours. Take out 40 g (1½ oz) to use as the next starter.

Pour the warm water into a bowl and dissolve the leaven. Add the flour and salt, and knead or slap and fold (see pages 177–78) for several minutes. Place the dough in a lightly oiled bowl and let it ferment for 2–3 hours until it doubles in size.

Divide the dough into 12 roughly equal parts of about 95 g (3¼ oz). Shape each part into a ball, creating surface tension, as you would in making bread. This part of the process is necessary for creating a pocket in the pita. Lightly flour, cover, and leave on a bench or tray to relax for 15 minutes.

Heat a pan or skillet to medium heat.

Take one ball at a time from under the cover, using a spatula or a scraper, and flatten it to form a circle on your floured work area with your hands or a roller. Aim for a circle no larger than 15 cm (6 in) in diameter. Don't make it larger, as if the dough is too thin there is a higher likelihood that it will rupture, which will burst your pita and any dreams of pockets.

Place the round flat dough on the dry, hot pan and fry for about 30 seconds. Wait to see bubbles forming on the top and flip to the other side with a spatula. Depending on the heat, flip again in 30–45 seconds. The pita should start rising and slightly yellow on both sides. Flip again, and let it fully inflate on the other side too. When the pita rises on both

(Continued on page 201)

sides, the pocket will be more even and easier to use without tearing. Flip until both sides are slightly brown (but not burnt), and set aside to cool down and deflate.

Often the pita needs some help to rise fully, and a spatula can help with this process. Gently and repeatedly push the pita against the pan, letting it rest for 5–10 seconds. When an air bubble starts forming, let it do its thing and see if it expands to the whole pita. If needed, gently squeeze it with the spatula, applying pressure to push the air bubble into the other areas of the pita. Sometimes repeated flipping also helps the pita to rise.

If you notice a gap where the steam bursts through, you can try to seal it temporarily with the spatula. Don't be discouraged if not all pitas rise and form a pocket. They will still be delicious and fantastic for dipping.

Pita can be stored at room temperature in a sealed container for 3–5 days or for 10 days in the fridge. Pita stores well in the freezer for up to 3 months in a sealed container. Allow it to thaw before heating. When using a pita from the fridge or freezer, heat it gently in a pan, oven, or toaster. Heating it will bring back its soft texture.

Tip: Creating a pita pocket

The factors that contribute to the rising of the pita, creating a pocket, and that you should pay attention to are:

- The sourdough starter should be active, and the dough doubled in size before dividing into balls.
- Balls should be shaped to have surface tension (see pages 178–80).
- The pan should be hot enough to encourage the moisture in the dough to steam, which pushes the dough upward.
- The pita dough should stay moist so it doesn't crack and lose steam when heated.

Sourdough Honey Challah

Makes 1 large six-braided loaf

Challah is the sweet, festive, and beautiful traditional Jewish bread eaten every Shabbat dinner, the weekly celebration of the arrival of the resting day. Making sourdough challah is not difficult, and it was how our ancestors had been enjoying it for centuries.

The challenge of making sourdough challah to meet modern palates is to reduce its sourness, which can be done by using a just-peaked leaven, rather than mid-peak, and controlling the fermentation time and temperature.

Different types of flour will affect the taste and texture of the challah. For instance, incorporating spelt flour, an ancient grain that pre-dates modern wheat, can lend the bread a nutty and somewhat sweet flavor. Spelt flour is also high in protein, fiber, and nutrients, which can make the bread more nutritious.*

This recipe doesn't require the dough to autolyse or to be folded as it ferments, and instead of scoring we will be braiding the challah. You can braid the challah into two smaller three-braided loaves rather than one large loaf, if you prefer.

This recipe is dairy-free but contains eggs.

DOUGH

25% — 150 g (5½ oz) leaven
40% — 240 ml (8 fl oz) warm water
13% — 80 g (2¾ oz) eggs (2 medium eggs)
10% — 60 g (2¼ oz) honey (or any sugar)
5% — 30 ml (1 fl oz) vegetable oil (we use sunflower oil)
2% — 12 g (⅖ oz) salt
100% — 600 g (1 lb 5 oz) flour (60% white wheat, 20% whole wheat, 20% spelt)

TOTAL HYDRATION CALCULATION

240 (dough) + 75 (leaven) + 80 (egg) + 30 (oil) = 425
425 (total liquid) / 675 (total flour) x 100 = 63% (hydration)

TO GLAZE

1 egg yolk
1 tablespoon water

TO DECORATE

1–3 teaspoons poppy or sesame seeds

---

* Georgia Frakolaki, et al., "Chemical Characterization and Breadmaking Potential of Spelt versus Wheat Flour," *Journal of Cereal Science* 79 (1 January 2018): 50–56, https://doi.org/10.1016/j.jcs.2017.08.023.

MAKING THE LEAVEN

Make the leaven in a 1:2:2 ratio—40 g (1½ oz) starter, 80 g (2¾ oz) flour, 80 ml (2½ fl oz) water. Leave it to ferment until the leaven has nearly doubled or just peaked. Don't let it mature further or it will over-sour the challah. Take 40 g (1½ oz) to use as your next starter.

MIXING

To a large bowl, add the water, eggs, honey, oil, salt, and then the leaven. Mix well. Add the flour and mix well. Once the dough is cohesive, place it on the work surface and knead for 5 minutes. Place in a lightly oiled bowl in a warm place, to begin bulk fermentation.

BULK FERMENTATION

During bulk fermentation, the dough will double in size. This could take 3–5 hours, depending on the room temperature and the strength of your starter.

SHAPING THE CHALLAH

Bring the dough to a wide surface, and divide it into 6 equally sized portions. You can use a scale to get more even results. Lightly flour the surface. You want to have the dough smooth and elastic and not sticky, so if needed, add 1 tablespoon of flour at a time, until you get the dough just right. Take each of the 6 chunks and shape them into long thin, even strands. See pictures overleaf. Now for the exciting part—the braiding process:

1. Place the rolls next to each other, and press them together at the top.
2. Cross the outermost two strands by first moving the outer left strand to the right, and then the outer right strand to the left side.
3. Move the outer left strand to the center (if you chose the wrong one, the first cross will unravel).
4. Move the second outer strand from the right to the outer left.
5. Move the outer strand from the right to the center.
6. Move the second outer strand from the left to the outer right.
7. Move the outer strand from the left to the center.
8. Repeat steps 4 to 7 until you get to the end.
9. To tidy the end, cut the last 3–5 cm (1¼–2 in) and press the strands together, or tuck the ends under the loaf.

Place the braided dough on a baking tray covered with parchment paper, which can be the same one you will use to bake it in the oven.

(Continued overleaf)

NOTES ABOUT BRAIDING

You can shuffle the strands of challah as you go to keep them at even spacing from each other, so it is clear where the relative position of each strand is.

Try to apply even pressure as you lift and move the strands, to avoid stretching and changing their length.

When first attempting to braid challah, don't hesitate to reshape your dough back to one ball and start again. With practice, you will learn to braid a beautiful challah in minutes. On the other hand, it doesn't need to look perfect to be delicious!

GLAZING

In a small bowl, prepare an egg glaze by mixing together the egg yolk and water. Brush the egg glaze on top of the braided dough, making sure to cover the whole surface and into the cracks. Keep the mixture in the fridge for re-applying another layer before the challah goes into the oven.

PROOFING

Cover the challah with another tray or a clean storage box and let the dough proof until it rises—doubling in size or close to it and feeling puffy. This can take about 3–5 hours at room temperature, or overnight at cold temperatures and in the fridge. Poke the challah to check that it is proofed (see page 181). Brush with a second layer of egg glaze, being a bit more gentle to not break the challah shape, which is more fragile now that the dough has risen. Sprinkle poppy or sesame seeds on top for decoration and extra flavoring.

BAKING

When the challah is close to finishing proofing, preheat the oven to 190°C (375°F).

As the challah is glazed, it does not need any steam. Place the challah in the bottom third of the oven, and bake for 40–45 minutes at 190°C (375°F). Halfway through the baking, you can rotate the challah to make sure it is evenly baked. If the challah starts charring, lower the temperature to 165°C (330°F) and add another 5 minutes to the baking time, or place a cover, such as aluminium foil, on top of the baking challah.

OUT OF THE OVEN

Take the challah out of the oven and let it sit on a wire rack for another 15 minutes before diving in. The challah will keep fresh in an airtight container or a sealed bag for several days.

Fermented Gluten-Free Buckwheat Bread

Makes 2 loaves

Buckwheat lends itself really well to fermentation, and since our friend Sarah Lily taught us how to make bread from fermenting whole buckwheat groats, we never looked back.

This exciting recipe has replaced all other methods we have used to make gluten-free sourdough bread. We love it, not only for its mild sour taste and great texture, but also because we are using NZ-grown buckwheat, making this a local gluten-free bread.

Buckwheat is a high-nutrient pseudocereal rich in proteins, flavonoids, and phytosterols. It is a valuable source of rutin, which shows anti-inflammatory, anticancer, antiatherogenic, and antioxidant activity.* In addition to making an awesome gluten-free sourdough, researchers recommend enhancing wheat bread and other baked goods with buckwheat thanks to its increased shelf life, high-value nutrition, and for having been shown to reduce blood glucose and insulin responses after its consumption when incorporated into white wheat bread.

A cool thing about this recipe is that it doesn't require a sourdough starter to raise the bread; instead, the yeast and bacteria come from the fermenting of the groats.

650 g (1 lb 7 oz) buckwheat groats

15 g (½ oz) salt

Place the groats in a 2 liter (70 fl oz) jar and fill up with enough water to cover the groats. Cover with a cloth or a loose lid and let the groats ferment for 2 days, mixing once a day. On the third day, drain the groats into a colander and rinse with water.

Place the drained buckwheat in a blender or food processor. Add the salt and blend for several minutes until a smooth and uniform batter is formed. Pour the thick batter back into the jar, and cover again with a cloth. Let the batter ferment at room temperature for another 24–36 hours. It will likely increase in volume by 10–20%, but don't hold back from moving to the next stage if it doesn't. Lightly oil two baking tins and pour the batter into them. Cover and leave for 4–6 hours or overnight. The bread may not rise during this time, but it will inside the oven, by 10 to 20%.

Preheat the oven to 190°C (375°F) for 20–30 minutes. Lightly glaze the bread with beaten egg or oil if you like, place a lid over the tins, and place in the bottom third of the oven. Bake for 40–45 minutes, removing the lid after 20 minutes of baking.

Let the bread cool down for 30 minutes, and enjoy. Once cooled, store in an airtight container at room temperature for up to 4 days or in the fridge for up to a week.

---

* J. A. Giménez-Bastida, M. K. Piskula, and H. Zieliński, "Recent Advances in Processing and Development of Buckwheat Derived Bakery and Non-Bakery Products—a Review," *Polish Journal of Food and Nutrition Sciences* 65, no. 1 (2015): 9–20, https://doi.org/10.1515/pjfns-2015-0005.

Fermented Gluten-Free Buckwheat Pancakes

Makes 10 medium pancakes

This recipe starts by fermenting buckwheat groats and blending them, just like in our buckwheat bread recipe (see page 206), to make delicious gluten-free pancakes. You can control how sour your pancakes will be by shortening or extending the fermentation time so that they can be enjoyed mild or soured.

Serve these pancakes with your favorite toppings. They pair incredibly well with fruit preserves such as Peach Sauce (see page 270) and Rose Honey (see page 284).

200 g (7 oz) buckwheat groats
250 ml (9 fl oz) water
5 g (⅛ oz) salt
Oil for frying

Place the groats in a 1 liter (35 fl oz) jar. Fill up with water to cover the groats, and cover with a cloth or a loose lid. Let the groats ferment for 2 days, mixing once a day. On the third day, you can decide whether to end the fermentation and make the pancake batter to enjoy them mild, or replace the water and let it ferment for another day or two for a sourer taste. Drain the groats into a colander and rinse with water.

Place the groats in a blender or food processor with the salt. Turn on and add 250 ml (9 fl oz) water in small amounts until the texture is smooth and the consistency is that of a thin pancake batter.

You can use this batter now or keep it in the fridge to use in the coming days.

Heat a heavy-based pan over a medium heat. Once hot, add a small amount of oil and pour a thin layer of batter of whatever size you enjoy. Fry the pancakes until bubbles appear and pop on the top side, then flip. The pancake is ready when it has browned on both sides. Replenish the oil as needed between batches, adding extra oil if you want the edges of the pancakes to crisp up. Stack the pancakes on top of each other and serve hot.

Sourdough Discard Pancakes

Makes about 15

The sourdough starter discard makes a delicious pancake, a concept we first heard about from our friend Gaz. We add eggs, salt, sugar, and water to make a sweet and sour pancake that everyone in our household enjoys.

250 ml (9 oz) discard starter
2 medium eggs
3 tablespoons sugar
¼ teaspoon salt
250 ml (9 fl oz) flour of your choice (optional)
Water
Sunflower oil for frying

In a bowl, mix the discard starter with the eggs, sugar, and salt. Add the flour, assess the consistency, and add water until the batter has a good pancake texture, on the runny side.

Heat a pan over medium heat. Add 1 teaspoon of oil, smearing it around the pan with a paper towel, and pour in the batter in batches to make small to medium pancakes. Taste the first one and see if you like it, and adjust accordingly.

Add oil as needed until all the batter is used up. Serve warm. Delicious with both vanilla and chocolate Crème de Marrons (see pages 271–73)—and did anyone say ice cream?

Yemeni Kubaneh

Makes 1 kubaneh in a 2.5 liter (88 fl oz) pot, or 8 kubaniot

Kubaneh is a big, soft and delicious Shabbat morning food for Yemeni Jews.

Niva's dad makes kubaneh with a family recipe passed on from his mother and her mother before her for generations. Preparation starts on Friday evening and the kubaneh bakes on low heat overnight, ready to be served in the morning with freshly grated tomato, Yemeni Green Schug (see page 280), and boiled eggs.

Kubaneh is the food that we would bring to school if asked to bring a family cultural dish, and we have always been a proud proponent of it being the best of all the (many) Yemeni pastries, even though it's a lesser-known one. Once, when Niva's father wasn't able to make the kubaneh to take to school, a family friend and neighbor Shuli came to the rescue. Shuli's kubaneh was different, rolled up into spirals and sprinkled with nigella seeds, and Niva remembers thinking it was very fancy.

We've included two recipes here, one of the kubaneh that has been made by Niva's family, who came from rural north Yemen. This recipe requires the use of a tight-lidded ovenproof pot, to stop the rising dough from overflowing into the oven. The other, known fondly as "kubaniot" (little kubanehs), uses rolling techniques, like Shuli's kubaneh. It originates from the communities in the south of Yemen. This option can be made in an unlidded baking dish.

Kubaneh is usually made with white flour, and it is really the tastiest option. We've also made it with organic white spelt flour with good results.

KUBANEH DOUGH

76% — 380 g (13½ oz) leaven
40% — 200 ml (7 fl oz) lukewarm water
100% — 500 g (1 lb 2 oz) white wheat flour
25% — ½ cup sugar
2.2% — 15 g (½ oz) salt
1% — 5 g (⅛ oz) black cumin (nigella seeds) (optional)

FOR OILING

80 ml (2½ fl oz) Samnah (clarified butter; see page 274)

TO SERVE

Eggs, at least 1 per person
Grated tomatoes
Yemeni Green Schug (see page 280)

FEEDING THE STARTER

Because we want a strong young starter, to reduce acidity in the recipe we feed it before making the leaven. Feed with a ratio of 1:1:1 which will give you 120 g (4¼ oz) starter. Take out 40 g (1½ oz) for your next starter.

(Continued overleaf)

MAKING THE LEAVEN

Once the starter is bubbly and active, use the remaining 80 g (2¾ oz) to make a 1:2:2 leaven and feed it with 160 g (5½ oz) flour and 160 ml (5¼ fl oz) water.

PREMIX

In a bowl, add the water and the leaven, and mix well. Add the flour and mix. Let it rest for 30–45 minutes.

MAKING THE DOUGH

After the premix has rested, add the sugar, and knead the dough until it is smooth.

KNEADING

Kneading of kubaneh dough is done while wetting the hands as necessary; this keeps the dough soft but stops it from sticking to your hands. Set a small bowl of water next to your kneading bowl for easy reach. Your dough should feel nice and soft, but not too liquid; if it is, add flour and only wet your hands if the dough is really sticky.

As you knead, pull up the dough from the bottom of the bowl and run it through your fingers to smooth out any lumps on its way down to a stretch and fold over the top (see page 178). Repeat the action while turning the bowl around to reach different parts until the dough is free of lumps.

Add the salt and the nigella seeds, if using, and knead them in, then cover the bowl and leave it to rise until it has doubled in volume.

BULK FERMENTATIONS

Kubaneh goes through two bulk fermentations. Once the dough has doubled for the first time, knead and fold it again, letting it rise to double the volume a second time.

Shaping, proofing, and baking

OPTION 1 — MAKE A BIG KUBANEH IN A TIGHT-LIDDED POT

A specialized pot is normally used for this, but we use an ovenproof 2.5 liter (88 fl oz) stainless steel pot with a tight-fitting lid, which works just fine. A flat lid is the best because it makes flipping the kubaneh easier, but you'll be fine in any case.

Oil the pot with melted samnah—use a whopping 80 g (2¾ oz) to both oil all over, and have a pool at the bottom.

Divide the dough into 5 soft balls.

(Continued on page 215)

With samnah-oiled hands, one by one place the balls into the pot, rolling each one in the samnah then placing them next to each other, one ball in the middle and the other four around it. Let the balls rise until they fill up three-quarters of the pot. This takes about an hour. Cover with a tight lid.

In a separate pot, boil the eggs.

Place the kubaneh pot into a preheated oven at 180°C (350°F) and bake for 45 minutes until the top is golden and the sides are firm and it is stable enough to flip. Take the kubaneh out of the oven and, using the lid and a plate, flip it back into the pot with the top now facing the bottom. Place the boiled eggs, still in the shell, on top of the kubaneh, and shut the lid. Leave the kubaneh with the eggs in the oven overnight at 100°C (200°F).

In the morning, it should be hot and tasty.

Serve with grated tomatoes, green schug, and peeled roasted eggs.

OPTION 2 — MAKE KUBANIOT IN A TALL BAKING TIN

We like to use a round cake tin to retain the traditional round shape of kubaneh, but an English cake tin works just as well. Or bake in a pot with a flat lid, same as the kubaneh, to get a "kubaneh m'fftaleh" like Shuli's. Oil the pot or tin with samnah.

Divide the dough into 8 balls. On an oiled surface, stretch each ball into a flat sheet (see the pictures on page 213). Oil the sheet with samnah, fold it into thirds, and roll it up. Twist the roll into a knot and place each rolled-up ball next to each other. Let them rise for another half hour in the baking pan.

Preheat the oven to 180°C (350°F).

Bake the kubaniot for 45 minutes until the top is golden. Check for readiness; if the dough is still wet in the bottom or inner rolls, flip and leave for another hour in the oven at 100°C (200°F), or until the kubaniot are cooked all the way through.

Once cooled, pull apart each kubanit as an individual serving, accompanied with grated tomatoes, boiled or roasted eggs, and green schug.

Amazake Bread

Makes 1 loaf

When we first made sweet amazake bread we were so impressed by how well it rose, the lovely texture, and the fact that it was mild and not even a little bit sour. We like making the bread just with amazake, though some bakers prefer to combine the amazake with sourdough to obtain the benefits of both.

58% — 260 ml (9¼ fl oz) warm water
15% — 90 g (3¼ oz) sweet barley amazake (see page 228 for instructions on how to make sweet amazake—replace chestnuts with barley)
1.4% — 6 g (⅛ oz) salt
100% — 400 g (14 oz) flour (50% white wheat, 50% whole rye)

In a bowl, place the water, amazake and salt and mix well. Add the flour, and knead together (see page 177) until everything is well mixed and you have a cohesive dough. Place in a lightly oiled bowl. Bulk ferment with no folding.

Shape the loaf and proof it in the bread tin. There is no need for scoring, but you can if you like.

Preheat the oven to 240°C (475°F).

Bake the loaf for 30 minutes with a lid over the tin (see page 182) or steam. Remove the lid and reduce the oven temperature to 220°C (425°F). Bake for another 15 minutes.

Take the bread out of the oven once the crust has colored to your satisfaction and place on a rack to cool.

Koji &
Miso

This chapter focuses on koji, a powerful mold whose domestication is as ancient as the domestication of rice, as far as 9000 years ago in China. Foods using koji are common in many East Asian cuisines and come in a great variety of methods and flavors, most notably in the production of alcohol such as sake, and the preparation of soybean to make miso and soy sauce.

The first thing Niva's friend Chika Morita ever said to her, as she approached her at the Thames Organic Shop, was "I heard you might want to learn how to make miso." She wasn't wrong. It was 2014 and we had just recently moved to the area; this was the first moment of a close friendship that started with Chika's passion to share her Japanese culture, and that has aged and matured like the many batches of miso that we have since laid. Chika has introduced us to the art of inoculating koji without an incubator, and to making with it a variety of delicious food from Japanese cuisine. Since then Chika has moved to the South Island where she sometimes teaches Japanese cooking workshops, so look her up if you are out that way.

Koji produces dozens of enzymes, of which amylases (which break down and liquefy starches) and proteases (which break down protein into polypeptides and single amino acids) are the most critical for koji applications. Thanks to its enzymatic activity it acts as a digestive aid.

Koji is also a prebiotic for multiple probiotic bacteria in the gut. Consuming koji or koji-based food has a multitude of additional potential benefits such as for skin conditions, the prevention of cardiovascular disease, hyperlipidaemia, and more.*

Today, people around the world enjoy growing and using koji. As its reach continues to expand, so does the variety of food made with it. In a large part these new recipes continue to follow the traditional process originating from East Asia and, more significantly, Japan, while incorporating different ingredients. There are also interesting new applications coming out from kitchens around the world, some of which we include

* Hiroshi Kitagaki, "Medical Application of Substances Derived from Non-Pathogenic Fungi *Aspergillus oryzae* and *A. luchuensis*-Containing Koji," *Journal of Fungi* 7, no. 4 (24 March 2021): 243, https://doi.org/10.3390/jof7040243.

in this chapter. Koji can be inoculated onto and hydrolyze any available starch into simple sugars, and its enzymatic power used to break down any protein, which opens the door to endless possibilities.

Over the years, we have experimented with a variety of applications. But it wasn't until we dived into the work of authors Rich Shih and Jeremy Umansky that we really got to see just how broad and varied the ingredients for koji-driven processes can be.

In this chapter we share some classic recipes as well as some modern takes. If you want to really drill into the ins and outs of the wide scope of possible applications with koji and the science behind these processes, we highly recommend reading Shih and Umansky's *Koji Alchemy*.*

Sourcing Koji Kin (spores)

There are many variants of koji molds out there, each with its unique characteristics. For the recipes in this book, and as a good starting point into koji-growing, you need to source white or yellow *Aspergillus oryzae*.

Each gram of koji kin makes a whole kilogram of koji—therefore a single purchase, kept cool, dry, and sealed, will last you for a long run. We have stored spores for years in the freezer and had no issues, though koji manufacturers don't recommend it because of the possibility of humidity going into the bag. If despite knowing the risk you choose to store your spores in the freezer or fridge, make sure they are properly sealed, and properly dry before reopening them.

White koji kin is considered the most beginner-friendly. It produces a good generalist koji, and is especially good for short application and does not tint or add color to the recipe. It is suitable for all the recipes in this book.

As of the time of writing this book there is no local supplier of koji kin, the spores used for making koji, in Aotearoa. We buy white *Aspergillus oryzae* koji from Japanese providers on eBay and there are plenty to choose from. You can also get yellow *Aspergillus oryzae* koji from Koji and Co in Australia, which also ships to New Zealand, and from Etsy.

As you grow your confidence you might want to experiment with other variants beyond white and yellow. In any case, we highly recommend buying koji kin that is produced by a recognized Japanese manufacturer, where production is well regulated, removing the risk of contamination from wild, toxic molds.

---

* Rich Shih and Jeremy Umansky, *Koji Alchemy: Rediscovering the Magic of Mold-Based Fermentation* (White River Junction, Vt: Chelsea Green Publishing, 2020).

Santizing for koji

With the high risk of contamination, both because of working with mold and because of protein spoilage risks, when working with koji and with any recipe using koji, we go beyond clean and into sanitized surfaces, counters, utensils, and containers. We use a food-grade sanitizer on anything touching or in proximity to our incubation setup and our fermenting area, as well as the containers and weights used to hold our koji-based recipes. You can also use high-percentage alcohol, such as vodka, instead of sanitizer. Ingredients that are used in koji preparation are heat-treated by cooking, steaming, roasting, toasting, etc. Basically, the areas of our house and kitchen that are used for koji applications are off-limits unless your hands are clean and intentions are pure.

Because of the high enzymatic activity, recipes using koji are reactive to metal, so opt for glass, ceramic, and food-grade plastic for anything touching them for a sustained time.

Pearl Barley Koji

Makes 1.2–1.5 kg (2 lb 10 oz–3 lb 5 oz)

Koji is traditionally grown on rice to produce kome-koji, or on pearl barley to produce mugi-koji (mame-koji uses another variant of the spore that grows directly on beans).We have often grown koji on basmati rice, which we usually have in the pantry. Rice koji is especially great for making light-colored preparations such as sweet white miso. We also enjoy using pearl barley, which produces a very hearty koji. It is delicious in amazake and as the base for vegetable miso. This recipe is written for pearl barley but whether you choose to make kome-koji or mugi-koji, the process is ultimately the same.

1 g (0.03 oz) koji kin
10 g (¼ oz) rice flour
1 kg (2 lb 4 oz) pearl barley
Water

DISPERSING THE SPORES

It only takes 1 g (0.03 oz) of koji kin to inoculate 1 kg (2 lb 4 oz) of barley, but that 1 g (0.03 oz) needs to be evenly distributed.

To make distribution easier, mix your koji spores with rice flour in a ratio of 1:10. We usually make two or three times that to use for multiple koji-growing purposes.

Use 10 g (¼ oz) of this dispersed rice-koji for 1 kg (2 lb 4 oz) of barley (following the method below).

When mixing, be careful not to breathe in the fresh spores. Tip them carefully from the bag to the jar, adding the rice flour on top. Close with a lid and shake.

We have kept dispersed koji in a tightly sealed jar in the fridge for weeks with no issue.

SOAKING AND STEAMING THE BARLEY

Soak the barley in water for at least 4 hours, or overnight. Rinse the barley until the water runs clean.

Place it in a steamer lined with a cloth (you can use a kitchen towel, diaper cloth, unbleached calico, etc). Shape the barley like a crater, to make sure there is no excess heat accumulating in the center. Steam for about half an hour, until the barley is cooked all the way to the middle, but before it turns soft and mushy. The goal is to keep each grain separately intact. If you are using rice, steam it until you see that the rice is translucent all the way through; it will take a bit longer, about 45 minutes to an hour.

(Continued overleaf)

PREPARING FOR INOCULATION

Spread the barley on a piece of cloth on a non-reactive tray such as a food-grade plastic or stainless-steel tray. Cedar wood is the traditional choice. We keep our layer at around 3 cm (1¼ in) thick. A thicker layer will generate more heat and, as a result, the temperature will keep shooting up and require constant mixing and tending to. A long period of overheating can also induce sporulation and spoilage. With our incubation setup, it means we are limited to making no more than 1.2 kg (2 lb 10 oz) of mugi-koji at a time.

Cool the barley to body temperature, occasionally mixing by running the barley between your hands to get rid of any clumps, being careful not to break the barley grains. Once cooled, sprinkle the dispersed koji powder evenly on the barley. The goal is that every grain comes in contact with the inoculate. Stir carefully, again avoiding breakage. Cover the barley with a damp piece of cloth to avoid condensation inside the incubation setup from dripping onto it.

For the next 36–48 hours the koji needs to be incubated in a humid environment, at 27–35°C (80–95°F). It is helpful to use a thermometer to keep track of the koji temperature; however, with time you should be able to feel if it is too hot or cold even with your bare hands. If the koji has a fever, it is too hot.

There are many ways to achieve an appropriate incubation environment. Since we live off the grid, we use a non-electric solution, but if this is not a barrier for you, there are simple schematics to follow online using heat pads, aquarium heaters, and other low-heat sources that can provide a stable environment.

If you are off-grid, you can keep the koji warm in your kitchen with simple aids such as hot-water bottles and an insulation blanket or a duvet. This is the method we have learned from Chika and have used for many years.

Here is how we do it. We place our tray on a rack to maintain good air circulation, then tuck our koji tray and rack into a big multi-layered/lined paper bag (the kind that wholesale dry goods come in) to retain the humidity. Then we add insulation and warmth as needed to keep it at the right temperature. We place hot-water bottles under the paper bag, and wrap the whole thing with an insulation blanket or a duvet. We have never needed to supplement humidity beyond the initial damp cloth cover, but if you are in a dry environment you will need to add a container with water or a humidifier to your setup.

Whichever way you choose, your role in the next 2 days is to make sure no part of the koji gets too hot or too cold. This is achieved by shifting the barley in the middle of the tray toward the edges and the barley in the edges toward the middle. The first mixing happens 6 hours in, with the following ones happening around every 12 hours. As you mix the koji, make sure to gently get rid of any clumps to encourage more even growth. After 36 hours, keep stirring if necessary, but you won't need to unclump it any longer, as the koji will be caking and turned into one mat.

With an off-grid setup, you will need to add additional temperature-regulating check-ins. They may include adding heat by refilling water bottles or, in the case of excess heat, additional mixing and ventilating such as leaving one side of the incubating setup open to cool down, or even taking the tray out altogether onto a sanitized benchtop.

In the first 24 hours keeping things hot enough is the main focus, but once colonization has kicked in, the energy that is created in the hydrolysis process that breaks complex carbohydrates into simple sugars produces plenty of heat. At this stage, the koji can get very hot very quickly, and no extra heating is required. A meat thermometer that can be set up to alarm you if the koji is overheating is a useful aid to have at this stage. To help cool your koji down, make furrows in the koji to increase its surface area; this traditional technique is useful at any scale.

You will smell the koji working before you can see it; it smells sweet and delicious.

Once the koji has fully colonized the barley, forming a mat of mycelium all through, it is ready. If you continue incubating it for too long the koji will bloom and spore.

Place the koji in the fridge to cool down, and get going with making something yummy with it from the following recipes. You can also keep koji in the freezer in a tightly sealed or vacuum-sealed bag.

Roasted Chestnut Koji

Makes approx. 1 kg (2 lb 4 oz)

As mentioned in the introduction to this chapter, koji can be grown on any available starch, including dehulled and polished grains (to allow the hypha access to the nutrients), premade foods (such as bread, pasta, and even popcorn), kūmara (sweet potatoes), and our favorite, chestnuts.

We harvest 1–2 tons of chestnut a year on the farm, which we sell fresh in season and also peel and freeze to use throughout the year. We love incorporating chestnuts into our dishes, both savory and sweet, and for us they are the most available source of starch.

To get chestnuts ready as a koji substrate we have found that they need to be oven-roasted, otherwise they will turn too wet and the koji will not establish properly.

We have used moistened chestnut koji as a bread starter in place of a sourdough starter, as a co-ferment by making a chestnut koji mead, for Shio Koji (see pages 232–33) and more. We absolutely love the sweetness that they provide in short applications such as amazake (see pages 228 and 231).

1 kg (2 lb 4 oz) peeled chestnuts (about 1.2 kg/2 lb 10 oz fresh in-the-shell nuts)
10 g (¼ oz) dispersed koji kin (see page 221)

Blanch the peeled chestnuts in boiling water for a few minutes. Once the chestnuts are warm, break them along their natural parting lines into halves, then roast them in the oven to the point that they are nice to eat and fairly dry (but not fully dehydrated). Cool to a comfortable handling point, then break up into smaller chunks. Make sure they have enough form to maintain individual integrity and some air gaps between them.

Inoculate and incubate following the process described in the Pearl Barley Koji recipe from “Preparing for inoculation” onward (pages 224–25).

Chestnut Koji Sweet Amazake

Makes 700 ml (24 fl oz)

Making amazake, a sweet fermented drink, is one of the nicer ways to enjoy fresh koji. Sweet amazake is made by combining koji with more cooked starch and incubating at 60°C (140°F) for 10–12 hours.

Ratios of koji to starch vary from recipe to recipe, but according to the experiment Sandor Ellix Katz describes in his book *The Art of Fermentation*,* the differences mainly impact the length of incubation time required. In our case, we are aiming for shorter incubation since we are using a food thermos or an insulation blanket and hot-water bottles to maintain the temperature over time.

This recipe is for making amazake with chestnuts. We follow the same recipe for our barley amazake and, like many other recipes in the book, you can use other ingredients with similar starch properties.

Chestnut amazake's nutty sweet flavor really comes through and is an awesome treat on its own. Barley amazake is delicious served with a bit of coffee or topped with cacao nibs (as pictured here). Sweet amazake is really very sweet, so it can be added to smoothies and desserts with no additional sweetener needed. Amazake is also a starting point for making alcohol and vinegar, and can also be used as a sweetener in baking, as a bread starter, and as a curing and pickling agent for vegetables and meats.

150 g (5½ oz) peeled chestnuts (about 180 g/6¼ oz fresh chestnuts)

Water to cover

300 g (10½ oz) chestnut koji (see page 227)

Place the chestnuts in a pot, cover with water, and boil until they are soft and mushy. Strain the cooking liquid into a measuring cup and keep 300 ml (10½ fl oz)—top up with more water if necessary. Cool down to 60°C (140°F).

Add the chestnut koji and reserved cooking liquid to the cooked chestnut mash and mix well. Warm the mixture back up to 60°C (140°F).

Transfer to a food thermos rated for at least 12 hours, or use a regulated incubation environment to keep at 60°C (140°F) for 10–12 hours.

If you want to use amazake's enzymic power for further applications, refrigerate it in a tight container. If you are planning to enjoy amazake as is, and want to increase its stability, you can bring it to a boil with a bit of water before refrigeration or freeze it for later use.

---

* Sandor Ellix Katz, *The Art of Fermentation: An In-Depth Exploration of Essential Concepts and Processes from Around the World* (White River Junction, Vt: Chelsea Green Pub, 2012).

Kohlrabi pickled in
Sour Amazake brine

Sour Amazake

Makes 1.2 liters (40½ fl oz)

Sour amazake is a mixture of koji, cooked starch, and water, left overnight at room temperature.

You can separate the liquid from the amazake and use it as a stand-alone fridge pickling brine for vegetables.

Use either sweet or sour amazake to marinade and cure meat.

300 g (10½ oz) koji
300 g (10½ oz) cooked barley or other starch
600 ml (21 fl oz) water

Mix all the ingredients together and warm up to 60°C (140°F). Pour into jars, seal tight with non-metallic lids, and leave overnight at room temperature or in a cooler.

Stored in the fridge, this will keep for many weeks.

Shio Koji

Makes 650 g (1 lb 7 oz)

One of the simplest and oh-so-versatile things you can make with koji, shio koji is a fermented mix of koji and salt water. Stable, yet packed with enzymes, it is perfect to marinate meat, and can tenderize tough cuts. It is also used in marinating fish and seafood as well as to add flavor, thickness, and richness to any savory dish in place of straight salt. You can pre-flavor your shio koji by adding herbs, spices, and even flowers in the preparation stage; keep in mind your end use, when you do. For example, we added 10 g (¼ oz) of sage to this recipe for shio koji that we used to marinate roasted chicken. You can be as creative as your garden and your imagination affords.

300 g (10½ oz) koji
5%–13% salt of the total weight (approx. 30–60 g/1–2¼ oz)*
300 ml (10½ fl oz) water

Break down the koji by rolling it between your hands to get rid of any clumps. Mix in the salt and gently squash together, or use a blender or food processor for a smoother texture. Add the water and leave in a cool spot.

Stir daily for 1 week, then weekly (or more in summer) while it is fermenting. When all the bubbling stops, it is done.

Kept in the fridge, shio koji lasts for ages.

*** *Note on salt***

Depending on your preference, the more salt you use the longer it will take to be ready, but the final product will have a longer shelf life. The less salt, the quicker the shio koji is ready and the final product will have a more balanced sweetness to the saltiness.

A higher salt ratio is traditional and was the original recipe we were taught at the beginning of our koji journey. Use this high-salt shio sparsely by replacing 1 tablespoon of salt with 2 tablespoons of shio koji in any recipe.

However, contemporary conversations around shio koji have highlighted the benefits of lower-salt shio koji; for example, you can use larger amounts of it as marinade without having to wash it off. As it has a nice balance of saltiness and sweetness, we really like the resulting low-salt shio koji.

The risk with lower-percentage shio koji is a higher production of alcohol and, as a secondary process, acetone. Mixing it daily should help prevent this from happening. Some people even go lower, making funky and flavored shio koji with as little as 2 percent salt. At what point is a recipe no longer the same recipe? We are not sure.

We encourage you to experiment, keep records, and make up your own mind, or make different shio koji for different purposes. Have fun.

Chestnut
Sweet Miso
13/10
Chestnut
Tamari
2022
Pinto
Tamari
2022
Kūmara
Tamari
2022

Miso

It would probably not come as a great surprise that there are many different types of miso, distinct from each other by length of aging, types of koji used, ratios of koji, salt, and beans, inclusion of other ingredients, and more.

We follow a simple, general division—as does Ellix Katz*—between short, sweet miso, which is ready in a few weeks; and aged miso, which can take a year or more to reach its desired maturity.

Generally speaking, sweet miso is lighter in color and, as the name implies, sweeter. It is ready within 4–12 weeks, a very short time compared with aged miso, and requires a higher proportion of koji and a lower proportion of salt. Sweet miso recipes can use as little as 4 percent salt of the overall weight of the koji, mixed with cooked protein. Higher proportions of salt content, around 7 percent, are also common (as is anything in between).

The dark and rich aged miso, on the other hand, needs a higher proportion of salt to stay safe over the long aging period—it takes a year or more to be ready. Aged miso requires less koji, as the enzymes have time to work over the long haul.

When making miso the weight used to weigh it down after packing into the container should be pretty heavy and cover the surface of the paste. Its job is to keep the miso compressed and avoid air bubbles as the miso gases out. As an alternative to using our standard fermenting weights we also use sealable bags filled with salt.

When you come to harvest your miso, you are likely to find mold growing on the surface. Unlike with most other ferments, if you have followed the sanitation and salting instructions you can just scrape this mold away, then discard the salted top layer and enjoy the miso below.

Over the aging period and again when you are ready to harvest the miso, you might find a liquid pooling at the top. This is tamari; decant it into a bottle to use as you would soy tamari or soy sauce. We usually try to leave headspace in our container especially so that we do not lose this delicious by-product.

Aged miso is shelf-stable, but sweet miso is kept refrigerated once you are happy with its flavors, or even frozen for long-term storage.

---

* Sandor Ellix Katz, *The Art of Fermentation: An In-Depth Exploration of Essential Concepts and Processes from Around the World* (White River Junction, Vt: Chelsea Green Pub, 2012).

Sweet Miso

Recipe for 4 liter (140 fl oz) container

Sweet miso is a great starting point when you first enter the world of miso-making. Unlike aged miso, you can make small amounts at a time. The high ratio of koji to protein makes the process faster and the low percentage of salt means you can use it more generously than aged miso.

This recipe uses locally grown organic pinto beans, a light-colored bean that makes a nice "white" miso. You can use any other legume in place of pinto beans and also any other source of protein, including animal proteins. Remember that every type of bean or protein will lend its flavor to the final product so this will not taste exactly the same as a traditional soybean miso, but it does share its wonderful salty, creamy, and umami characteristics.

700 g (1 lb 9 oz) dry pinto beans
Water
85 g (3 oz) salt, plus extra to layer on top
1 kg (2 lb 4 oz) koji (see pages 223–25)

Soak the beans in water overnight, then cook by boiling gently in fresh water until they are soft. Drain well, reserving the cooking water. Once the beans and brine are cool enough to handle, mash the beans, using a potato masher for a chunky paste or a food processor for a more even texture.

Take 2 cups of the reserved cooking water and dissolve the salt in it.

Break down the koji carefully by rolling it between your hands to unclamp, then mix it with the salt water and cooked beans.

If the miso mixture is hard, add a bit more liquid so it's shapeable. It should be soft and moist all through, wet but not dripping. There is a bit of flexibility as a bit more water can give you more tamari, though there is a higher risk of acetone formation in the miso.

Pack tightly in a sanitized container by throwing handfuls into the container, so that at impact any air bubbles are removed (if you ever built with cob, this would feel very familiar!). Cover the top with a layer of salt to deter unwelcome microorganisms. Weigh down heavily. Clean the tops of the container with sanitizer and paper towels so that there are no droplets or smears above the salt line. Cover with a tight cloth or a loose non-metallic lid.

You can start tasting your miso for readiness after 4 weeks. Discard any surface mold and the salt layer. If you want a very smooth miso, this is the time to blend it. Transfer your miso into smaller containers to keep in the fridge.

If 12 weeks have passed and you think your miso needs more time aging, let it! Many people continue to age their sweet miso beyond the traditional point.

Veggie Miso

Miso, particularly sweet miso, can incorporate many other ingredients. Anything added to this process will transform to add new and interesting characteristics to the paste. We love preserving vegetables from the garden into miso and find that the possibilities are endless and the results delicious.

There are two main types of vegetable miso we make. The first is vegetables mixed with pulses, seeds, or grains. Since most vegetables do not contain much protein, adding them to a legume-based miso makes a lot of sense. We use NZ-grown lentils and unblended pearl barley (mugi) koji to complement the meze/salad direction we want our mixed vegetable miso to take.

The other type is stand-alone vegetable and koji miso. Popular choices include summer squashes (including the seeds) such as butternut, and garlic. We enjoy making a kūmara (sweet potato) miso and also globe artichoke, which is higher in protein than most vegetables and tastes amazing mixed into tahini.

Made with a short fermentation in mind (4–6 weeks) and a low salt proportion (4 to 5 percent), both types can be enjoyed in cooking as well as as a spread, a dip, or as part of a sauce.

Vegetable miso also produces tamari, so don't miss out on harvesting this unique liquid before you decant your miso jars.

All the recipes we give you on the following pages follow the same process—the vegetables and lentils are cooked or roasted until soft and then blended before being mixed with the koji and salt and fermented following the instructions for Sweet Miso (see opposite).

From top: chestnut and rice koji miso, Sweet Miso (page 238), Globe Artichoke Miso (page 242), Zucchini Salad Miso, Kūmara Miso (page 242), Roasted Beet Miso, Aged Miso (pages 243–45)

Roasted Beet Miso

Recipe for 4 liter (140 fl oz) container

This miso is a gorgeous color, making it a lovely and surprising addition to any meal. We pick our beet straight from the garden and opt to roast the long, beautiful red stems too.

400 g (14 oz) cooked lentils
170 g (6 oz) roasted beet and beet stems
700 g (1 lb 9 oz) pearl barley (mugi) koji (see pages 223–25)
5% (63 g/2¼ oz) salt

Mash together the lentils and beet. Once the mash is cool enough to handle, mix with the koji and salt. Follow the instructions for Sweet Miso (see page 238) to ferment.

Zucchini Salad Miso

Recipe for 2 liter (70 fl oz) container

One of the cool things about miso is that you can make it from excess food you happen to have. In this recipe, an excess of zucchini salad (containing one onion, three zucchinis, and a handful of mint) was cooked and incorporated into a lentil miso. Mixed with olive oil before serving, this miso is perfect on a slice of bread.

300 g (10½ oz) cooked lentils
300 g (10½ oz) cooked zucchini salad
600 g (1 lb 5 oz) pearl barley (mugi) koji (see pages 223–25)
4% (48 g/1¾ oz) salt

Mash together the lentils and zucchini salad. Once the mash is cool enough to handle, mix with the koji and salt. Follow the instructions for Sweet Miso (see page 238) to ferment.

Globe Artichoke Miso

Recipe for 2 liter (70 fl oz) container

Artichokes have two to three times more protein than most vegetables and make a very interesting stand-alone miso. We grow a lot of artichokes as they make a fantastic hedge plant. While we love devouring pots full of artichokes dipped in salad dressing, there are times where there is just more than we can eat. Making globe artichoke miso is one way that we use surplus artichokes in season. Serve mixed into tahini; no extra salt or lemon needed.

700 g (1 lb 9 oz) cooked artichoke hearts and other soft parts (be extra careful not to get any hairs in)
1050 g (2 lb 5 oz) pearl barley (mugi) koji (see pages 223–25)
4% (70 g/2½ oz) salt

Boil or steam artichokes until the leaves separate easily. Pick off the leaves and scoop away the hairs from the inside of the hearts. Enjoy the bits of artichokes on the leaves or scrape them off to include in the recipe.

Mash the artichoke. Once the mash is cool enough to handle, mix with the koji and salt. Follow the instructions for Sweet Miso (see page 238) to ferment.

Kūmara Miso

Recipe for 2 liter (70 fl oz) container

Of course we had to make it! Kūmara (sweet potato) miso is a yummy sweet, salty, and saucy miso, best eaten young.

465 g (1 lb ½ oz) kūmara (sweet potatoes)
535 g (1 lb 3 oz) pearl barley (mugi) koji (see pages 223–25)
4% (40 g/1½ oz) salt

Cook or roast the kūmara until soft, then mash. Once the mash is cool enough to handle, mix with the koji and salt. Follow the instructions for Sweet Miso (see page 238) to ferment.

Aged Miso

Recipe for 10 liter (2.25 gallon) container

Ready in one year, much better after three years, aged miso is a whole other level of experience. Rich and deep, this dark paste is so worth the wait.

We enjoy using a variety of pulses for our miso, driven by what is locally grown and which organic beans or proteins we can source at the time of preparation. Chika, on the other hand, always prefers to use traditional soybeans for her aged miso, and if they're not available, opts for black beans, especially for achieving the specific depth of flavor she is after for her three-year-aged batches. As always, we encourage you to try it for yourself and make up your mind.

Miso years are measured in summers—the end of each summer the miso aged through is one year. But we've found that with the mild summers in Aotearoa, aging miso takes more time.

We usually make big batches of aged miso, at least 4 to 10 kg (8 lb 13 oz to 22 lb) at a time, and age them for at least three years. We contain it in a 10 or 20 liter (2.25 or 4.5 gallon) food-grade bucket, and use an inverted plate that fits neatly in the bucket as a lid, with a jar of salty water for extra weight. We let our miso age in a cool part of the house, in our bulk pantry/storage area. After the first year (summer), we taste our miso regularly, every 6 months or so (if we remember!), and are often surprised to see how slow the process of getting that truly dark rich result we are after can be. Once the top layer has been taken off, we often find the inner parts still needing more time. But the wait is so, so worth it. When the miso is properly aged, it is divine. Don't forget to reseal and weigh down your miso after each check.

Since starting to make miso with Chika, we've always used the ratios in this recipe. However, recipes for aged miso vary according to the source, and many suggest using half this amount of koji. The overall idea is that given the time to operate, less koji is required, while the need to reduce the chance of contamination over a long period of time means we need more salt. Adding mature koji to the mix gives the microorganism community a start in the right direction.

(Continued overleaf)

2 kg (4 lb 8 oz) dry beans
Water
800 g (1 lb 12 oz) salt, plus extra to line container and layer on top
2 kg (4 lb 8 oz) koji
¼ cup mature miso

Soak the beans in water overnight, then cook by boiling in fresh water until they are soft. Drain well, reserving the cooking water. Mash the beans to your preferred texture.

Take 1 liter (35 fl oz) of the reserved cooking water and dissolve the salt in it.

Break down the koji carefully by rolling it in between your hands to get rid of any clumps and mix it with the salt water and cooked beans. Mix in the mature miso.

If the miso mixture is hard, add a bit more liquid so it is shapeable. It should be soft and moist all through, wet but not dripping. There is a bit of flexibility as a bit more water can give you more tamari, though there is a higher risk of acetone formation in these miso. Before packing into a sanitized container, salt its bottom and sides. Pack tight by throwing handfuls shaped into tight balls into the container, so that at impact any air bubbles are removed. Or layer and pack tightly, pressing down with your hands. Cover the top with a layer of salt to deter any unwelcome microorganisms. Weigh down heavily. Clean the tops of the container with a sanitizer and paper towels so that there are no droplets or smears above the salt line.

Cover with a cloth or a loose non-metallic lid.

When you are ready to harvest the miso, discard any surface mold and the salt layer. If you want a very smooth miso, this is the time to blend it. Transfer your miso into smaller containers. Aged miso doesn't require refrigeration.

Misozuke

Miso can be used for misozuke—the pickling of vegetables by layering them in a bed of miso (sometimes mixed with other ingredients such as sake or mirin). The misodoko—the miso or miso mixture used—can be reused several times to make more misozuke.

We like making misozuke with aged miso using vegetables that might be too hard to eat on their own, such as radish pods. We grow daikon radish as part of our cover crops and in our microgreens. That's why daikon grows and self-seeds in many areas in our garden. In the spring we have an abundance of easy-to-gather radish pods, and making misozuke out of them makes perfect sense.

Radish pods

Miso (enough to cover the pods)

Alternate layers of radish pods and aged miso in a non-reactive (plastic, glass, ceramic) container, making sure the pods are not touching each other. Cover with a non-reactive lid. While some vegetables can be enjoyed as misozuke after as little as a couple of hours, the tough radish pod misozuke is ready in 10 days.

Scrape the miso off the pods before serving.

Potato Miso Salad

Serves 10

This dish is so tasty and is a family favorite. Hearty and satisfying, this is an easy dish to serve at dinner or as part of a feast. We particularly like making it with a big bunch of mint, which brings a lightness to this otherwise grounded dish. Our favorite misos for this recipe are Aged Miso (see pages 243–45) or Zucchini Salad Miso (see page 241).

2 kg (4 lb 8 oz) potatoes, halved
1 heaped tablespoon miso
Olive oil to drizzle
Big bunch of seasonal greens (such as mint, parsley, scallions, and/or garlic chives), finely chopped

Boil the potatoes in a pot full of water until they are soft and their skins start to separate. Drain and place in a serving bowl.

While still hot, mix in the miso and drizzle olive oil over the potatoes. Mix through the majority of the greens and garnish with the rest.

Koji-Cured Vegetables

Koji-Cured Kūmara

Once you realize that koji grows on starch, the leap to trying it out on kūmara (sweet potatoes) is obvious for anyone growing their own and looking for a local starch source.

We have grown koji on kūmara for many years, enjoying the sweet result as sort of instant amazake. But it was only after reading *Koji Alchemy* (see page 221) that we realised that there was a potential for taking koji kūmara to a new level. The recipes in this section follows in the steps of their vegetable charcuterie method.

Kūmara, peeled — as many as can easily fit in your inoculation and dehydration setup
Salt — 2% of the weight of the cooked kūmara weight
1 sprig of rosemary and ½ bay leaf per kūmara (optional)
Dispersed koji to cover the kūmara (see page 223)

Boil the kūmara in a pot of water until they are cooked all the way through but are not yet soft. Drain, then cover with salt and the herbs if wished. Keep in a tightly sealed container in the fridge for a few days, 2–10 depending on the size of the kūmara.

Pat dry, inoculate with dispersed koji all around, and let it grow in your koji incubation setup for 36–48 hours until the koji has covered the kūmara and has matured well on it. Ideally, you will place the kūmara in a way that requires the smallest amount of surface area touching it—we have used colanders, racks, and dehydrator trays, and all of them worked fine.

Because of our off-grid setup we like to incubate a tray of koji at the same time, which, after the first 24 hours, maintains the temperature in the incubator on its own.

Dehydrate until the kūmara loses about 60% of its weight.

Enjoy thin slices on a piece of bread.

Broccolini Stalks "Jerky" (see page 252) with koji-cured kohlrabi, carrot, beet, purple kūmara, and golden kūmara.

Broccolini Stalks "Jerky"

At the end of the broccolini season, broccolini heads become smaller and smaller still, producing long edible stems with just tiny florets.

This is a great time to harvest those broccolini stems, cutting just above the point where they turn stiff rather than nice and bendy. We recommend harvesting as many as you can easily fit in your incubation setup as this process is quite involved and the result—a yummy jerky-like snack (see photo on page 251)—will be eaten up all too quickly.

Broccolini
Salt — 2% of the roasted broccolini weight
Smoked paprika — in a ratio with the salt of 3:1 (for 3 g/0.09 oz of salt add 1 g/0.03 oz of smoked paprika)
Dispersed koji to cover the broccolini (see page 223)

Preheat the oven to 220°C (425°F).

Spread out the broccolini stems on a tray and roast for about 15 minutes. Salt the roasted stalks with the mix of salt and smoked paprika. Place in the fridge in an airtight container for a couple of days.

Pat dry, inoculate with dispersed koji all around, and let it grow in your koji incubation setup for 36 hours, or until the stalks are covered with a layer of koji.

Dehydrate for a day. Snack on a whole stalk at a time!

Preserves

When we talk about preserves, the two key elements for us are a prolonged shelf life without the need for refrigeration, and great eating quality. Preserves help us take produce that could spoil in days or weeks and make it last years. Most of this chapter is focused on recipes of the kitchen staples we preserve through canning, one of the most important modern innovations for food preservation. We also included in this chapter Crème de Marrons (see pages 271–73), a sugar-based chestnut conserve, and Samnah or clarified butter (see page 274), a process that makes butter shelf-stable.

Canning basics

Canning is an important process that makes foods safe to store and consume for years after they have been made, while retaining the same eating quality as the day they were made. It is a method of preserving food in hermetically sealed containers (jars and bottles or, in industrial settings, cans) and sufficient heat processing to enable the food to be stored at room temperature or in the pantry. When preparing jars or bottles for canning, they should be cleaned with hot water and soap and rinsed well, but they don't need to be sanitized before filling them up with food or drinks, as they will be heat-treated in the canning process.

Depending on how many jars you will be using, you might choose to use any of the following solutions below to preserve your foods. Use one of these canning options after making the recipe, placing the contents in jars or bottles, and closing with a secured lid.

It is always better and safer to start the canning process while everything is still hot from pouring pasteurized food or liquid into the jars or bottles.

- Place jars and bottles inside a pot with water covering them entirely and bring them to a boil. Simmer on low heat for 10 minutes. We very much recommend using specialized tongs that securely hold jars, or a canning rack specifically made for this purpose, to avoid hot water splashing and potential burns.

Apple cores Vinegar 2021
Mint Jun Vinegar 2022
Peach Vinegar 2021
Mixed bean Miso
Mixed bean Miso

- Place jars and bottles in the oven at 130°C (250°F) for 20 minutes.
- Place jars and bottles in a solar cooker at a temperature of 65°C (150°F) for 1 hour.

Jars

Use jars that are heat-proof and can handle scalding temperatures. These can be newly bought or you can reuse jars that previously contained preserves.

Glass doesn't respond well to a quick increase in temperature, and pouring scorching foods and drinks into a cold jar will likely cause them to break. Avoid jars cracking by gradually heating them before filling them with hot preserves, such as rinsing them with warm water or using them straight from the dishwasher after a hot cycle.

A trick we use (that works almost every time) is to pour only a minimal amount, 1–2 cm (½–¾ in), of the hot food into several jars, and then return to the first one and fill it up.

When filling jars, it is best to give them a slight tap or two once full, to release any air bubbles. If needed, use a spoon or spatula to clear bubbles inside the jar.

Lids

When working with preserves, use lids in good condition that are not damaged and have no exposed metal or rust. Damaged lids might not make a good seal and can lead to air entering the jar or bottle, which can contaminate your creation. If a lid has a good shape but has exposed metal, you can cut a square piece of parchment paper and place it between the jar and the lid.

When tightening lids, screw lids and bands securely, but if you are especially strong, not as tightly as possible. If the lid is fastened too tightly, air cannot vent during processing, oxygen will remain inside the jar, and this will cause discoloring and earlier spoilage during storage. Over-tightening could also cause lids to collapse and jars to break, especially with raw-packed, pressure-processed food.

When placing lids, ensure the jar's top is clear of food residues. If needed, use a damp paper towel to clean off the food item to create a better seal.

As jars cool, the contents in the jar contract, pulling the self-sealing lid firmly against the jar to form a high vacuum. This also means that screw bands are not needed on stored jars and can be removed once the jar has cooled.

It is best to make a habit of checking that the lid is secure once the content has cooled down and any screw bands have been removed. We usually let the jars cool down on the kitchen bench and check the lids before moving them to the pantry.

Occasionally a seal will not form, and while the contents can still be enjoyed, it will not store. If this happens to a significant amount of jars, you can repeat the canning process using other types of jars and lids. Otherwise, move this item to the fridge and consume it within a week.

Headspace

Air expands significantly more than food when heated to high temperatures. The higher the temperature, the greater the expansion. As canning exposes food to high temperatures, ensure a headspace of 2.5–3 cm (1–1¼ in) between the contents and the lid.

Food safety notes when canning

A significant health risk of *Clostridium botulinum* poisoning, known as botulism, can occur when preserving hot foods. ***Firstly, don't fill hot food into a jar without continuing the process by pasteurization*** using one of the canning methods on pages 258–61.

Don't smell, touch, or eat any food from jars that looks or smells bad, or from jars that are damaged, cracked, leaking, swollen, or squirt liquid or foam when opened.

Clostridium botulinum is unable to grow in foods that have a high acid content, such as most fruits, or when exposed to oxygen. Therefore, the bacteria and toxins are most often associated with home-canned foods with low acid content, such as vegetables and meats, that have not been properly processed.

When opening a jar of low-acid preserves, such as tomato sauce, meats, soups, and vegetables, it is best to boil and cook the contents for 10 minutes, as botulism can be present without apparent signs.*

Low-acid foods are considered those with a pH higher than 4.6. In many cases, adding lemon juice or vinegar before canning will assist in lowering the pH below this level, in foods that otherwise would have a higher pH than 4.6.

Preserves are best consumed within two years of canning. While many preserves will keep well for several years, they will keep losing about 20 percent of their vitamin content per year. During prolonged storage they can also experience deterioration in flavor, texture, color, and nutrients. Label the jars with the date of the canned preserve to ensure you use older preserves first.

---

* "National Center for Home Food Preservation | USDA Publications," accessed 17 February 2023, https://nchfp.uga.edu/publications/publications_usda.html#gsc.tab=0.

Preserved Tomato Base

Makes 6 liters (210 fl oz)

Anyone who grows tomatoes knows there is always a time in the season when there are simply more fresh tomatoes on the kitchen bench than can be eaten. Tomato sauce is one of the most classic preserves and, homemade or bought, it continues to find its way into most kitchens.

There are many approaches to making tomato sauce, some requiring peeling and sieving, while others, like the recipe below, take a more laid-back approach resulting in a chunkier sauce. We like to make our tomato sauce with onions, as there is hardly ever a time when we don't want them included in a dish.

This tomato base is best used as an ingredient in cooking, as in Spicy Shakshuka (see page 266), soups, stews, pasta sauce, or reduced as described in the Homemade Pizza Sauce recipe (see page 269).

2 tablespoons olive oil
1 kg (2 lb 4 oz) onions, diced or sliced
1½ tablespoons salt
7 kg (15 lb 7 oz) tomatoes

In a large pot, heat the oil and sauté the onions on low to medium heat until they become translucent. Add the salt and stir through. Add the tomatoes and bring to a slow boil, stirring regularly. Simmer on low heat with the lid off for 45 minutes, stirring occasionally.

Follow the canning instructions on pages 258–61.

Optional

If you have bell peppers and chilies handy, you can add them to this recipe to enjoy a slightly different but equally delicious sauce.
1 kg (2 lb 4 oz) bell peppers
3–6 chilies, to taste
¼ cup sweet paprika

Spicy Shakshuka

Serves 5 (2 eggs per person)

Shakshuka is the result of a delicious combination of tomato sauce and eggs. From this essential starting point, endless variations are possible and, indeed, are found in kitchens around the world. Simple additions such as herbs and spices, chili, Preserved Lemons (see page 287), feta cheese, and also fish are common takes on this much-loved dish around the Mediterranean and the Middle East.

Making shakshuka from scratch is easy enough in season: start by caramelizing the onions, then add fresh tomatoes to make a sauce. But out of season, or if you're in a hurry, using Preserved Tomato Base is an as-easy-as-it-gets solution for a hearty meal.

In Yemen, shakshuka sauce is seasoned with a spice mix called hawaij, and added garlic and chili. We are inspired by the hot and aromatic flavors of Yemeni shakshuka, using Yemeni Green Schug (see page 280) as a quick way to introduce both chili and garlic and quite a few spices found in hawaij. We've also been enjoying a teaspoon of grated ginger in our shakshuka, which gives this shakshuka a refreshing twist.

In Yemen, the eggs are scrambled into the sauce, but while we do often make delicious saucy scrambled eggs like this as a quick brekkie, for special meals we love our shakshuka eggs poached, with the runny yolks mopped up by soft challah bread.

2 tablespoons olive oil
500 ml (17 fl oz) Preserved Tomato Base (see page 264)
2–3 teaspoons Yemeni Green Schug (see page 280) (use more or less to make it hotter or milder)
1 teaspoon grated fresh ginger
10 eggs
½ cup chopped fresh parsley to garnish

Heat the oil in a cast-iron pan. Add the tomato base and mix in the schug and ginger. Bring the sauce to a boil.

Once boiling, reduce to a simmer and add the eggs, one at a time, to the sauce, using a spoon to make room in the sauce by pushing it a bit to the side for each egg before placing it in. Cover with a lid and simmer on low to medium heat just until the egg whites turn opaque but the yolk is still runny.

Garnish with parsley and serve with challah (see pages 202–5), pita, or bread of your choice.

Homemade Pizza Sauce

Makes sauce for 5 medium pizzas

As we make large amounts of Preserved Tomato Base (see page 264), we have been using it in various recipes and found that with a mild adaptation it makes for a fantastic pizza sauce. In this simple recipe, we add a bit of oregano for its excellent accompaniment to pizzas, a bit more salt, which always upgrades a pizza, and cook it over low heat to get a thick sauce that spreads beautifully on a pizza base (see photo on page 194).

1 liter (35 fl oz) Preserved Tomato Base (see page 264)
2 sprigs of fresh or dried oregano
5 g (⅛ oz) salt

Pour the tomato base into a wide, heavy-based pan, add the oregano sprigs, and bring to a slow boil. Reduce to a simmer and cook for about 30 minutes. Stir regularly to avoid the sauce burning on the bottom of the pot and to allow for better evaporation of excess water.

Once the sauce has got close to being thickened to your satisfaction, let it cool down to room temperature, which will thicken it a bit more. This will store up to 5 days in the fridge.

Summer Vegetables Preserve

Makes 2 liters (70 fl oz)

This is another great recipe that preserves the richness of the summer garden. We use this throughout the year, mostly in stews and soups. You can add other spices and herbs, though we prefer to keep it relatively simple so it will be a versatile addition to future dishes.

2 tablespoons olive oil
8 medium to large onions, diced into large chunks
2 large eggplants, diced
1 teaspoon ground black pepper
5 g (⅛ oz) salt
15–20 tomatillos, quartered
2–3 medium zucchinis, sliced into rounds
1–2 fresh chilies, chopped (optional)

Place a large heavy-based pot on medium heat, and add the olive oil and onions. Stir regularly and cook for about 5 minutes before adding the eggplants and black pepper. Cook for about 20 minutes, stirring regularly. Add the salt, tomatillos, zucchinis, and chilies, if using, and cook for 10 minutes. Dispense into jars and can (see pages 258–63).

Peach Sauce

Makes 3 liters (105 fl oz)

We have a very happy purple peach tree growing in our chicken coop. With the access to nutrients, it's thriving and regularly provides bumper crops of peaches. We have several more peach trees that we grew from seed and there are others growing around the garden that self-seeded, so peaches are our most abundant summer fruit. As a result, we make many liters of this peach sauce every summer. And every winter, we enjoy it with both sweet and savory meals. We don't usually add sugar to our sauces, just a tiny bit of honey to balance the acidity. We find peach sauce perfect as a topping for pancakes (see page 209), and we also use it regularly as a dip for farm sausages. It is an excellent ingredient for desserts and a perfect companion for meat. This recipe works with many other fruit. Strawberry sauce (pictured on page 260) is another household favorite of ours.

4 kg (8 lb 13 oz) peaches
1 cup water
1 tablespoon honey
¼ teaspoon salt

Leave the skin on the peaches or, if you prefer, you can peel them. Slice the peaches, remove the pits, and place them in a heavy-bottomed pot. Add the water and bring to a slow boil, stirring regularly to promote even cooking and avoid burning the bottom. Once boiled, reduce the heat to low. Cook for about 40 minutes with no lid, or partly open to allow water vapor to escape, stirring occasionally. The peaches should be soft and partly dissolved, with some chunks still intact. If you prefer a more solid consistency you can reduce the cooking time to only 20 minutes, or increase it to 1 hour for a more homogenous texture and no chunks. You can also make this recipe in a slow or solar cooker. If so, double or triple the cooking time until you reach the desired texture.

Take off the heat, add the honey and salt, and mix well.

Pour into glass jars (a little bit at first, so as to not crack the jars) and secure with a lid. Follow with canning as detailed on pages 258–63.

Crème de Marrons (Chestnut Conserve)

Makes 800 ml (28 fl oz)

On our farm, there is a beautiful mature chestnut orchard that our farm partners planted in the early '90s. We enjoyed oven-roasted chestnuts in our childhood and during our travels in France and Italy in all the marvellous ways they are served there. We spent some time in Ardèche, France, in our early twenties. This region of France is particularly known for its chestnuts and its original Crème de Marrons, and so, we got hooked.

Chestnuts differ from most other nuts by having a relatively high carbohydrate portion and a lower fat ratio. This makes chestnuts best used fresh. Chestnuts reach peak sweetness within a week of falling from the tree and don't keep well out of refrigeration. If stored at low temperatures of 1–4°C (34–40°F), they will keep for 2–3 months.

We use chestnuts lavishly when they are in season, and we also peel large amounts—at our scale, we have a small, dedicated peeling machine—and freeze them to be used later in the year in stews, soups, pan-fried, and in bakes.

We love using chestnuts to make Crème de Marrons. This recipe captures the unique creamy, thick texture and the sweet, nutty flavor of chestnuts. It is less sweet than traditional recipes, as we refined it to use less sugar, but it is still shelf-stable and can be used throughout the year.

We have two versions of this recipe that we relish eating: the more traditional vanilla-flavored and another with cacao (we love cacao). The process is similar for both recipes, but the results are significantly different. As the two versions are delicious, we have included them both here.

Use like any spread—on toast, pancakes, crepes, as a tart filling or glaze in desserts.

750 g (1 lb 10 oz) chestnuts in the shell or 500 g (1 lb 2 oz) peeled chestnuts
water

VANILLA-FLAVORED
CRÈME DE MARRONS

250 g (9 oz) sugar (any kind)
180 ml (5¾ fl oz) strained liquid from cooking the chestnuts
1½ teaspoons vanilla extract
1 g (0.03 oz) salt

"CHOCOLATE SPREAD"
CRÈME DE MARRONS

335 g (11¾ oz) sugar (any kind)
100 g (3½ oz) cacao
250 ml (9 fl oz) strained liquid from cooking the chestnuts
1 teaspoon vanilla extract
1 g (0.03 oz) salt

(Continued overleaf)

PREPARE THE CHESTNUTS

First, we cook and then extract by cutting in half and scooping out the chestnut flesh from the peel, or peel the chestnuts before cooking.

To cook and then peel, rinse the chestnuts, place them with the peel intact in a pot, and cover with water about 2 cm (¾ in) above the chestnuts. Bring to a boil, lower the heat to a simmer, and cook for 45 minutes. Strain the chestnuts, and save the water for adding later on. Let the chestnuts cool to a temperature that is still warm but comfortable enough to handle. Cut each chestnut in half and, using a teaspoon, scoop the flesh out of the shell.

To peel the chestnuts raw, cut off the top and bottom ends, and make another cut across the shell (from top to bottom). You can then easily remove the chestnuts from their jacket (shell). You will notice the chestnuts have another protective layer, the pellicle—it is nutritious and safe to eat. Place in a pot, cover with water, bring to a boil, then lower the heat to a simmer and cook for 30 minutes. Drain, saving the liquid.

MAKE THE CRÈME DE MARRONS

Depending on which flavor Crème de Marrons you're making, blend the chestnut flesh with the relevant ingredients and continue to blend until homogenized and no small chestnut pieces can be seen.

Slowly bring the mixture to a boil in a pot, then cook for another 10 minutes on low heat, stirring constantly so the sauce doesn't burn and the air bubbles burst.

While the Crème de Marrons is still hot, dispense it into jars and follow up with canning (see pages 258–63). Expect your Crème de Marrons to keep for a year in the pantry. Once opened, keep in the fridge and use within 5 days.

Samnah

Makes approx. 400 ml (14 fl oz)

Samnah is clarified butter, common around the Middle East. It is one of the most important oils in Yemeni cuisine. The advantages of samnah over butter are that it doesn't require refrigeration and it is friendlier to those who are lactose intolerant. This Yemeni samnah recipe adds another layer of flavor using fenugreek seeds; ½ teaspoon gives enough flavor to the samnah without becoming overpowering. Fenugreek is the prime flavoring used in "maple flavored" products thanks to its delicious aroma, which makes this samnah excellent for both sweet and savory dishes. Keep in mind that in higher proportions, the sweet fragrance of fenugreek will make its way to your sweat glands, making you smell like a maple flavoring factory!

½ teaspoon fenugreek seeds (optional)
500 g (1 lb 2 oz) butter

In a hot saucepan or pot, lightly roast the fenugreek seeds for just a few seconds.

Place the butter in the pot on the lowest heat possible, without a lid. As you cook the butter, you will notice that a foam develops on the surface. This foam contains protein and should be skimmed off. Keep on heating until no more foam develops, but instead big bubbles of clarified butter come to the surface, and any remaining milk solids stick to the bottom. Let the samnah stand for a couple of minutes so that any floating sediments settle to the bottom.

Pour the samnah carefully into clean jars through a sieve to catch the fenugreek seeds. Avoid pouring the milk sediments from the bottom of the pot. Seal the jar with a lid, and store in the pantry away from direct light.

If any jars develop a white sediment at the bottom after a few minutes, you can transfer the samnah carefully to a new jar, leaving those sediments behind. If any foam is visible on the top of the jar, skim it out before sealing. You can add a tablespoon of uncooked rice to the pot when cooking the butter, to help settle more milk solids in the bottom. This rice can be later enjoyed by dairy-eating friends or fed to the chickens or compost.

Condiments

This chapter includes several recipes that are eaten as condiments that did not quite fit anywhere else.

Preserved lemons, for example, is a delicious condiment that is not quite fermented but rather, as the name suggests, a preserve, and its low acidity and high salt content is the key to its long shelf life. Interestingly, research on a similar lemon preparation has found them to have very low microorganism activity, dominated by yeast.*

Schug, both red and green, have their shelf life extended due to their potent mixture of chili and spices, though they still require refrigeration. Those spices, including garlic, cloves, coriander, and cardamom,† have been shown to have antimicrobial properties that inhibit harmful food-borne bacteria, yeasts, and mold growth.

Honey is a preservative all of its own, and rose honey is a delicious example of capturing seasonal flavors and aroma with it. These recipes are so good, we simply couldn't leave them out.

---

* Hammoumi Aayah, et al., "Characterisation of the Dry Salted Process for the Production of the Msayer, a Traditional Lemon Aromatising Condiment," *LWT—Food Science and Technology* 43, no. 3 (April 2010): 568–72, https://doi.org/10.1016/j.lwt.2009.09.005.

† R. R. Chattopadhyay, et al., "Herbal Spices as Alternative Antimicrobial Food Preservatives: An Update," *Pharmacognosy Reviews* 1, no. 2 (2007): 239–47.

Yemeni Green Schug

Makes 300 ml (10½ fl oz)

Green schug was the hot condiment of Niva's childhood. Niva's grandma, Hava, would go to the market to buy the fresh cilantro and chili to make green schug as tradition requires, at home. Growing up, we would add green schug to anything and everything, from soups, to omelette batter, in cheese sandwiches and, most importantly, mixed with grated tomato on the Saturday mornings when Niva's father Eitan baked Kubaneh (see pages 211–15). Of course, green schug was also part of a quick lunch with flaky malawah and other Yemeni pastries and dishes.

The exact ingredients of schug change from family to family. This recipe is based on what Niva recalls from her grandma's recipe, along with what others who have made schug with her shared with us.

2 heads garlic
4–5 green chilies (we use jalapeños)
2 large bunches of cilantro (approximately 180g/6¼ oz), roughly chopped
1 teaspoon ground cumin
5 g (⅛ oz) salt
1 teaspoon ground cardamom
2 cloves

Place all the ingredients in a food processor, and pulse until the ingredients are evenly ground into a slightly chunky mixture.

Place the schug that you won't be using on the day in a container with a tight lid. Kept in the fridge, schug will store well for up to 2 months. During this time, due to oxidation, the color will change from light green to a dull dark green.

Green
Schug
01/23

Yemeni Red Schug

Makes approx. 150 ml (5 fl oz)

Red schug is green schug's hotter sibling and, you've guessed it—it is red. Made with dried red chilies, it is easy to make in small batches year-round, and with the added heat, a small jar can last for quite a while when refrigerated.

We use cayenne chilies, as we love growing them. Use milder (or hotter) red chilies to suit your preferences.

50 g (1¾ oz) dried cayenne chilies, tops cut off
1 cup water
2–3 cloves garlic, peeled

SPICE MIX
¼ teaspoon coriander seed
¼ teaspoon ground cumin
¼ teaspoon black peppercorns
4 cardamom pods
3 cloves
¼ teaspoon salt
15 g (½ oz) fresh cilantro

Soak the chilies in the water for 2–3 hours.

Meanwhile, make the spice mix, using a spice grinder or a mortar and pestle to grind all the spices together.

Drain the chilies, keeping the water. Add the chilies, garlic, and spice mix to a food processor along with 2 tablespoons of the chili-soaking water. Pulse until all the ingredients are evenly ground into a slightly chunky mixture; add more chili water as necessary to achieve your desired consistency.

Pack into a small clean jar and keep refrigerated. Red schug will keep for up to 6 months in the fridge.

Rose Honey

Makes 1 liter (35 fl oz)

Rose honey is the easiest way for us to capture the short season in which our fragrant Damask roses are in bloom. Roses are rich in phytochemicals,* making this preserve both fabulous and nutritious. Damask rose is our favorite rose and has been used for centuries for food, medicine, perfume and cosmetics. It is the rose used in rose water and the main rose used in the cosmetics industry. You could use other fragrant roses, and even opt for varieties grown specifically for their suitability for eating because of their lower sourness, such as a fragrant hybrid tea rose like the flavonoid-rich "Mister Lincoln."†

Whichever rose you're using, pick them once the dew has dried off, to avoid adding excess moisture to the honey. Separate all the petals and remove any old or bad ones.

If you are making a bulk amount, it would be easier to mix all your honey and rose petals in a mixing bowl or food-grade bucket and transfer to jars later.

Rose honey is a highly coveted treat in our home. Once a jar is opened, it will be all gone all too fast, as it's everyone's preferred way to sweeten their hot drinks, add to yogurt, put in smoothies, and drizzle on desserts.

1 liter (35 fl oz) honey
1 liter (35 fl oz) rose petals

Add a layer of honey to the base of a clean jar, then push as many rose petals as you can into it. Repeat by adding another layer of honey and pushing in more rose petals. We use two long teaspoons or chopsticks to help poke the petals into the thick honey. Keep adding honey and rose petals until your jar is nearly full.

Let the honey infuse for a month. If you are using thick honey, placing it on the window sill can help accelerate the process. As the honey draws out the liquids from the rose petals, the honey will turn runnier and fragrant. Over time the petals float up; at this point, if you like, you can separate the top layer, which is thick with petals, from the bottom layer, which is now flavored runny honey, both of which are ready to use.

---

* Athrinandan S. Hegde, et al., "Edible Rose Flowers: A Doorway to Gastronomic and Nutraceutical Research," *Food Research International* 162 (December 2022): 111977, https://doi.org/10.1016/j.foodres.2022.111977.

† Haejo Yang and Youngjae Shin, "Antioxidant Compounds and Activities of Edible Roses (*Rosa hybrida* spp.) from Different Cultivars Grown in Korea," *Applied Biological Chemistry* 60, no. 2 (April 2017): 129–36, https://doi.org/10.1007/s13765-017-0261-4.

Preserved Lemons

Recipe for 500 ml (17 fl oz) jar

In this simple recipe we use salt to transform lemons to create a culinary treat. The preserved lemons are ready to eat as early as within three days, while also keeping for many years.

While you can use any lemon for this recipe, a variety with a medium-thick peel is ideal, to avoid the bitterness of excess peel.

The preserved lemon slices can be served on top of almost any dish, eaten as is, as a couple of slices inside a sandwich, or mixed into salads.

5 medium ripe and nicely yellow lemons
30 g (1 oz) salt
2 teaspoons paprika
Juice of 1 lemon
Olive oil, to seal

Slice the lemons into 5 mm (¼ in) slices and remove as many pits as possible; this will massively help reduce bitterness.

Mix the salt and paprika on a plate. Lightly touch one side of each lemon slice in the mixture, shake to remove excess salt, and pack into a clean jar. If you touch both sides of the lemon in the salt, it would be too salty. Even with one side, we are not going for full coverage—just for some of the spice mix to stick on. As you pack the lemons into a clean jar, the juice from the lemons mixed in with the salt will start rising up, acting as a brine.

Add lemon juice as needed so that the lemons are fully submerged. If any lemons are floating, use a clean weight to keep them down. Top with olive oil to seal and sit on the kitchen bench out of direct sunlight.

After opening, store in the fridge.

Amba Lemons

Recipe for 500 ml (17 fl oz) jar

This is a version of preserved lemons that uses amba spice mix instead of just paprika. If you have made Homemade Amba Spice Mix, don't miss making this delicious condiment. Use lemons with a medium-thick peel to reduce bitterness.

5 medium or 3 large ripe lemons
15 g (½ oz) salt
1 teaspoon Homemade Amba Spice Mix (see page 57)
Juice of 1 lemon
Olive oil, to seal

Slice the lemons into 5 mm (¼ in) slices and remove as many pits as possible, to help reduce bitterness.

Mix the salt and amba spice mix on a plate. Continue the steps as in the recipe for Preserved Lemons (see page 287).

Preserved Lemon Salad Dressing

Makes 300 ml (10½ fl oz)

This salad dressing is really something. The lemons cause the oil to emulsify into a velvety rich dressing that can pick up any salad. It is a great vegan alternative to mayo dressings. We enjoy dipping globe artichoke leaves in it as we make our way to the hearts. It's also exceptionally smashing when topping salads with hard-boiled eggs.

125 ml (4 fl oz) Preserved Lemons (see page 287), including the brine
¼ teaspoon black pepper
2 cloves garlic
¼ teaspoon ground cumin
50 ml (1¾ fl oz) sunflower or olive oil
1 teaspoon honey
125 ml (4 fl oz) water

Place all the ingredients in a blender or food processor and blend together on the highest setting until smooth.

Transfer to a jar and store in the fridge. The dressing thickens in the fridge. Use as is, or dilute to your preferred consistency.

Curing Meat, Tallow & Broth

Meat preservation has been a part of human culture since prehistory, and evidence of ancient salt curing is found around the world.

Whether you grow your own or buy your meat, we very much encourage knowing where the meat comes from. When sourcing meat, the best practice is purchasing local and grass-fed and, if possible, from where animals are grown on unsprayed (better yet, managed organically and regeneratively), perennial, multi-species pastures.

We are privileged to grow and enjoy meat from animals that live on green pastures and are killed on the farm. This connection helps us appreciate the life of these animals, and with respect to them, we use as much of the carcass as we can.

In this chapter, we start with the exciting practices of curing meats by various techniques, followed by a delicious liver pâté recipe and recipes for making tallow (fat) and broth.

Curing Meats

Most meat cuts are suitable for curing. Even the cheaper, tougher cuts will produce tasty, tender cured meats, as the curing process tenderizes the meat. This means we can easily use the tougher cuts and leave the more tender cuts to be used in other ways that highlight their quality. The most crucial factor when choosing a meat cut is to use only fresh meat and avoid meat near its expiry date.

Once the meat is cured and dried, it will keep for a substantial amount of time, meaning that this is a great food to take on trips or to just keep handy to be enjoyed as an easy, nutritious snack.

We make cured meat when we have a few relatively relaxed days, so we know we can dedicate our attention to following up on the recipe steps. It is an easy process but needs to be adhered to, as meat is a more risk-averse product to ferment and preserve. When we cure meat, we use a variety of natural food-preservation processes that, when combined, make a powerful preservative to ensure the meat is safe from unwanted contaminants, especially botulism.

We often make a large amount, which we divide into batches with different seasonings to enjoy over the coming weeks and months.

The natural preservatives at our disposal include vinegar, wine, honey, salt (at 2–3.5 percent of the meat weight), sugar, chili, pepper, and various condiments and herbs, which are also anti-microbial. Lastly, we finish with the drying process, which, combined with the salting, reduces the water activity in the meat and leads to a combined effect of osmotic pressure and structural stress that together reduce microbial activity and make the meat unsuitable for pathogens to proliferate.*

A kitchen scale is very handy for making cured meats, as getting the correct ratios of the various ingredients, salt to meat in particular, is a crucial part of making them safe and delicious.

We are happy to use cuts that have some fat in them. As the fat dries and absorbs flavors, it becomes delicious. We have found that in our home, the cuts with the fat get eaten much faster than the leaner cuts. The downside is that fat spoils faster. If you use meat cuts with a significant amount of fat, they will be best kept in the fridge and consumed within a few weeks. Using leaner cuts, or trimming the fat from your fattier cuts, will increase the shelf life of your cured meats to several months and more. If you plan to store your jerky or biltong in the fridge and use it within a few weeks, most cuts will do, and we recommend leaving at least a bit of fat for it to enrich your cured meat flavor. Common cuts we use are topside roast, bottom side roast, round roast, chuck, and blade.

It took us many years to get up the bravery to cure meat. When we started our fermentation journey, something about it intimidated us and we didn't want to take risks. But cured meats are a lot simpler to make than we initially thought. After attending a meat curing workshop with Brad King of Falls Retreat, it seemed within reach, and our fridge has been in regular use to cure meats from the animals we grow on the farm.

Curing meats is not a one-step recipe, but it is definitely not rocket science either. It involves trimming a piece of meat, marinating, draining, rubbing spices, and placing it on a rack in the fridge for it to dry. Then the meat can be stored and enjoyed whenever the occasion suits.

---

* Samuel C. Watson, et al., "Fate of *Escherichia coli* O157:H7, *Salmonella* spp., and *Listeria monocytogenes* During Curing and Drying of Beef Bresaola," *Meat and Muscle Biology* 5, no. 1 (30 April 2021), https://doi.org/10.22175/mmb.11621.

Air-dried Cured Meat (Bresaola Style)

Makes 400–650 g (14 oz–1 lb 7 oz)

We love making bresaola, a relatively simple meat-curing recipe that transforms fresh meat into delicious dry-cured meat. With a bit of effort, making this recipe at home from relatively cheap cuts will allow you to enjoy top-quality cured meats without the high price tag.

While bresaola originates from Italy, cultures around the world have made similar cured meats, with variations including the cut of meat used, the type of animal, the flavoring, and the curing time.

Bresaola will enrich your cuisine with unique flavors and textures and can be served and enjoyed on platters and charcuterie boards, in sandwiches, on crackers, as pizza toppings, or as a side dish.

The equipment required is simple and should be found in your kitchen: you'll need a bowl, strainer, and a rack that the meat can be placed on with air circulating under it (a small oven or bread rack works well).

The total time you should expect to prepare and process this recipe should be about 1 hour, followed by the curing and drying period that altogether should take between 4 weeks and 3 months.

1 kg (2 lb 4 oz) sheep, beef, deer, goat, or pig meat
500–750 ml (17–26 fl oz) wine and/or vinegar mix (see Marinading on page 300)

We suggest two different spice mix rubs we love using when curing meats. The recipe is the same for both mixes.

SPICE MIX #1

2% sweet or smoked paprika (20 g/¾ oz)
1% black pepper (10 g/¼ oz)
0.5–1% garlic — 0.5% dried (5 g/⅛ oz) or 1% fresh (10 g/¼ oz)
0.5% dried chili (5 g/⅛ oz)
0.1% allspice (1 g/0.03 oz)
3% salt (30 g/1 oz)
2.5% coconut sugar (25 g/1 oz)

SPICE MIX #2

1% black pepper (10 g/¼ oz)
0.3% dried garlic (3 g/0.09 oz)
0.2% chili (2 g/0.06 oz)
0.2% fennel seeds (2 g/0.06 oz)
0.5% roasted coriander seeds (5 g/⅛ oz)
0.4% ground cinnamon (4 g/0.12 oz)
0.2% ground fenugreek (2 g/0.06 oz)
3% salt (30 g/1 oz)
2.5% cane sugar (25 g/1 oz)

(Continued on page 300)

PREPARING THE MEAT AND WEIGHTING

Prepare the meat by trimming off large pieces of fat if present, and any loose meat parts that might significantly increase the surface area of the meat. The meat cut should be "tight" so the rubbing mix can cover the whole surface.

Measure the weight of the meat you will be curing. If your piece is larger or smaller than 1 kg (2 lb 4 oz), this will help match the amount of salt/sugar/spice mix you will be rubbing onto the meat. The weight will also indicate when your meat is thoroughly cured and dried.

If possible, cure the meat as one or two large pieces. If you use steak cuts or other relatively thin pieces, opt for pieces not less than 2.5–3 cm (1–1¼ in) thick, so as not to lose the beautiful grain, texture and color in the middle of the cut once it is cured. Note that you might need to increase the amount of your rubbing mix as there will be more surface area. Don't increase the salt quantity but add more of the other spices if needed.

MARINADING

Once the meat is prepared, place it in a bowl that will contain it and the liquid that will cover it. You can use any type and ratio of wine and vinegar. Leftover wine or mead sitting in the fridge is our first choice, which we will then top up with vinegar to reach full coverage. This mix is the first method of preserving the meat while enriching it with flavor.

Ensure the wine and vinegar mix covers the meat completely without air pockets. Cover and leave in the fridge for at least 6 hours and up to overnight.

PREPARE THE RUBBING MIX

To get the most flavor from your spices, source them whole and crush them with a mortar and pestle or a spice grinder, before mixing with the salt and sugar. If using coriander seeds, we suggest lightly roasting them in a pan to release more of their aromatic flavor.

Once the mix is made, separate it into two parts—about three-quarters to use on the first rubbing and one-quarter to use a few days into the process. Place the one-quarter portion in a jar inside the fridge.

DRAINING AND RUBBING

Drain the liquid from the meat. You can pat it dry, but we don't tend to do so. The meat should not be wet but still moist enough for the rubbing mixture to stick to it.

Place the meat in a clean bowl, and rub the three-quarters portion of the rubbing mix on evenly. Pay attention to getting into all the meat folds, so the entire surface is covered with the rubbing mixture.

Place the meat in a clean and dry sieve or colander and place it in the fridge, uncovered, with a tray or bowl underneath to capture the draining liquids.

TURNING AND RE-RUBBING

Turn the meat daily for 5–7 days so the meat dries evenly and quickly from all sides.

Sometime on day 3 or 4, take the meat out into a bowl, and rub in the last quarter portion of the rubbing mix that you had set aside. Once done, place the meat back in the sieve and let it sit there.

DRYING

After 5–7 days, the curing process is complete. The next stage is to continue to dry the meat, preferably slowly and evenly so the surface doesn't form a hard crust, which would lock moisture in. The meat should slowly dehydrate right through, improving its flavor, texture, and storability. We prefer to wait at least 3 weeks but enjoy it more after 2 months.

While professionals use very controlled and precise temperature and humidity levels, at home, we suggest drying the meat in the same setup you cured the meat in—a colander or rack inside the fridge, without a cover. The refrigerator keeps the cured meat at temperatures that will dry it safely and evenly. Most modern fridges have a fan to extract moisture, which helps a lot with the curing process. Turn the cured meat once every 2–3 days until it loses roughly half its weight or the occasion calls to start enjoying it.

If you want to use a dedicated fridge or curing chamber, or if you want to go for long-term drying of months and years, you can set your dedicated setup to a more accurate meat drying temperature and humidity to facilitate a more even drying and prevent a hard crust from developing. Set the temperature to 10–12°C (50–54°F). The humidity range will be best started at 80–90 percent for the first week and gradually dropped to 70 percent.

Other drying solutions include a dedicated cool box, an electric curing chamber, a dehydrator, or a smoker. A cool box should be netted from insects and rodents and placed in a dry, shady, ventilated location. This system works very well in the colder months of the year.

We prefer to dry cured meats on racks or sieves because it is simple and results in superb cuts of cured meats. Other options include setting up a rod, such as a round piece of wood, inside the fridge that meat can hang from, either with meat hooks or by tying the meat with twine, with or without covering the meat with cheesecloth.

It is ready once the weight has gone down by one-third. If you want to dry it more for better storage qualities, dry it until two-thirds of the original meat weight has been lost.

This cured meat style is best enjoyed when sliced thinly and is a bit translucent. To assist thin cutting, use very cold meat from the fridge and a sharp knife or slicer.

Jerky & Biltong

Another great way to cure meats is by processing beef into dry jerky and biltong. Jerky and biltong differ in origin as well as in other aspects, such as texture and flavoring. Both will dehydrate much faster than bresaola, and are brilliant to take on trips or as a quick snack at home or for the school lunch-box.

There's an endless array of flavoring mixtures to spice up your jerky and biltong, with jerky generally being sweeter and biltong more vinegary. We have included our favorite flavorings in the recipes following.

Drying your biltong and jerky can be done in a dehydrator, fridge, smoker, or oven. Traditional biltong is dried whole over several days at lower temperatures, which adds additional depth to the meat. Jerky is usually cut into smaller pieces and dried within a few hours, resulting in more of a meat preserve than a ferment.

Biltong

Makes 400–600 g (14 oz–1 lb 5 oz)

1 kg (2 lb 4 oz) beef
500 ml (17 fl oz) vinegar and wine mixed

SPICE MIX
2% (20 g/¾ oz) coriander seeds
1% (10 g/¼ oz) black peppercorns
0.5% (5 g/⅛ oz) cumin seeds
0.5% (5 g/⅛ oz) chili, or more for more heat
2.5% (25 g/1 oz) salt
2% (20 g/¾ oz) sugar

PREPARE THE MEAT

Prepare whole pieces up to 2 cm (¾ in) thick, trimming any loose meat. Don't hesitate to leave on fatty parts. A great thing about this recipe is that pretty much all the meat can be used, and while some slices will be smaller, they can still be cured and dried.

Measure the weight of the meat you will be curing. If it is more or less than 1 kg (2 lb 4 oz), this will help match the amount of salt/sugar/spice mix you will be rubbing onto the meat. The weight will also indicate when your meat is thoroughly cured and dried.

MARINADING

Once the meat is prepared, place it in a bowl that will contain it and the liquid that covers it. You can use any type and ratio of wine and vinegar. Leftover wine or mead sitting in the fridge will be our first choice, topping up with vinegar to reach full coverage. This mix is the first method of preserving the meat while enriching it with flavor.

Ensure the wine and vinegar mix fully covers the meat without air pockets. Cover and leave in the fridge to marinate. Biltong can be marinated for anything from 8 hours up to several days.

PREPARE THE RUBBING MIX

To get the most flavor from your spices, source them whole and crush them with a mortar and pestle or a spice grinder, before mixing with the salt and sugar. Lightly roast the coriander seeds in a pan before grinding to release their aromatic flavor.

(Continued overleaf)

DRAINING AND RUBBING

Drain the liquid from the meat. The meat should be dry but still moist enough for the rubbing mixture to stick to it. Place the meat in a clean bowl; use the rubbing mix and rub it evenly onto it. Pay attention to getting the spices into all the meat folds so the entire surface is covered.

DRYING

Place the meat on a rack or colander, or hang it. Biltong dries at 25°C (75°F) over a few days or in the fridge for up to a week. Turn the biltong once a day (not necessary if hanged). At any time you can stop the dehydration and eat any of the biltong pieces, which can be a good way to check on how the dehydration is going. Any reduction in volume will make delicious biltong, but for better storage you should look at a 50–60 percent reduction of its original weight.

When we estimate that we will eat the biltong within a few weeks, we often choose to dehydrate it to only about 40 percent reduction of the original weight, as that is our household preference.

Biltong can be stored outside of the fridge in cool, dark conditions for several weeks if the final weight of the meat is at 50 percent of the original weight or lower. A higher percentage could develop mold. If storing out of the fridge, keep the biltong in a paper bag to avoid trapping moisture.

Jerky

Makes 400–600 g (14 oz–1 lb 5 oz)

1 kg (2 lb 4 oz) beef
500 ml (17 fl oz) vinegar and wine mixed

FLAVORING MIX

¼ cup tamari or 30 g (1 oz) Aged Miso (see pages 243–45)
½ cup honey (or ¼ cup honey plus ¼ cup sugar)
4–6 cloves garlic
2.5 cm (1 in) piece fresh ginger
5 g (⅛ oz) chili
1 teaspoon ground black pepper

PREPARE THE MEAT

Prepare the meat by cutting it using a sharp knife, following the grain of the meat, into relatively even slices of 5–7.5 mm (¼–⅜ in) thickness and 1–2 cm (½–¾ in) width. An even thickness will allow the meat to dry consistently, which prevents some pieces from over-drying while others are not yet dry enough. You can ask your butcher to pre-slice the meat cuts for you at no extra cost, as they have precise machinery and can save you time and achieve better results. At home, use meat cuts that have been frozen and only semi-defrosted, as that will make cutting much more precise with less effort. Jerky works very well with steak and schnitzel cuts.

MARINADING

Once the meat is prepared, place it in a bowl that will contain it and the liquid that covers it. You can use any type and ratio of wine and vinegar. Leftover wine or mead sitting in the fridge will be our first choice, which we will then top up with vinegar to reach full coverage. This mix will be the first method of preserving the meat while enriching it with flavor.

Ensure the wine and vinegar mix fully covers the meat without air pockets. Cover the meat and leave in the fridge for at least 4 hours and up to overnight.

PREPARE THE FLAVORING MIX

In a bowl, mix together the tamari or miso and honey.

Crush or thinly slice the garlic, ginger, and chili and add them to the mixture along with the black pepper. Stir until all ingredients are evenly dispersed in the mixture.

(Continued on page 308)

Take the whole livers, rinse them and place in a bowl. Cover the liver with vinegar and leave in the fridge for at least 2 hours or overnight.

Drain the vinegar and prepare the liver by removing the outer membrane, which should peel easily. Cut out unwanted parts, which is anything but the liver meat. Remove the sinew and cut the liver into chunks about 2 cm (¾ in).

Add the onions, olive oil, and tallow to a deep pan or heavy-based pot. Cook for 5 minutes on medium to low heat, stirring regularly.

Add the thyme, rosemary, salt, pepper, chili, and garlic to the pan or pot and cook, stirring regularly, until the onions are evenly browned and caramelized.

Increase the heat to medium-high and add the brandy or other alcohol and the liver pieces. Stir regularly for 5 minutes until the liver is evenly cooked and is no longer red on the inside. Don't overcook the liver, as it will develop an off flavor and tough texture. Move the contents of the pan/pot to a bowl to slow further cooking.

When the mixture is at room temperature, add the honey. Place everything in a blender or food processor with the lemon juice and blend until the mixture is smooth. Taste the pâté and add salt if needed.

Transfer the pâté into clean jars. We usually use 100–250 ml (3½–9 fl oz) jars, which is an amount we will use in a week. Smooth the tops of the jars and leave about 2–3 cm (¾–1¼ in) of headspace at the top of the jar. This will allow you to add a thin layer of olive oil to the pâté to seal it and leave space for the pâté to expand in the freezer.

Keep one jar to eat and enjoy your creation, and place the rest in the freezer. The frozen pâté is best used within a year. Once opened, store in the fridge and use within a week. Serve on toast or crackers.

Tallow (Animal Fat)

Tallow is rendered (clarified) beef or sheep fat, also called dripping in the UK, where it's known to be served on bread or toast with salt and pepper—referred to as "bread and dripping." Animal fat is a by-product of butchering animals, and making it into useable cooking oil is simple and easy.

This traditional cooking fat plays a significant part in our kitchen. It is a local fat that is readily available, which we make when receiving the fat from the butcher who processes our home-killed animals. Beef, sheep, and pork fats can be purchased cheaply at your local butcher, but you might need to ask for some to be reserved for you.

Tallow can be stored in the pantry for several years and will be soft and easy to scoop out at room temperature.

Culinary aspects aside, tallow has other uses such as in pet food (we use it as a dog treat), candle-making, soap-making, waterproofing, as a lubricant for steel (it's great for oiling hinges), and for oiling tool handles. Tallow has a similar composition to the fat naturally produced by human skin, making it suitable for skincare products (we don't tend to use it in this way, though).

Tallow has been shown to raise cholesterol and makes rats gain more fat, so it should be consumed moderately. However, when looking at the accumulation of fats in the liver (fatty liver) and free-radical damage, tallow was much preferable to soybean oil.*

Depending on where in the animal the fat you are using comes from, the tallow will have a stronger or milder aroma. The color of the fat will also vary depending on the type of animal, the breed, the time of year, and the animal's diet.

Tip: Avoid pouring fat down your drain, to keep your plumbing in good health. Instead, scrape off as much fat as possible and finish off using a paper towel or other cloth.

---

* Akira Tajima, et al., "Is Beef Tallow Really Hazardous to Health?," *Nutrition Research* 15, no. 10 (October 1995): 1429–36, https://doi.org/10.1016/0271-5317(95)02015-N.

Tallow

We use tallow in many ways, especially for roasting vegetables, cooking or grilling meats, frying, deep-frying, and stir-fries. Tallow has a high smoke point of 249°C (500°F).

When making recipes using tallow, we prefer to serve them hot or warm, as when tallow cools down it hardens and is less appetising.

We like to use tallow for caramelizing onions, which is a base for many dishes. We also regularly mix olive oil and tallow in cooking, with the occasional splash of toasted sesame oil.

Beef or sheep fat

To prepare the fat for rendering, divide it into smaller pieces. This will allow moisture to escape and distribute the heat evenly, making the rendering process more efficient and quicker. It is easier to cut or mince fat when it is cold, so aim to use the fat straight out of the fridge or semi-frozen out of the freezer. Using a sharp knife, you can dice or cut the fat into pieces under 3 cm (1¼ in) and place them straight in a pot. You can also spend more time with the knife, chopping the fat into small pieces, or even mince it in a food processor. Recently, our friend Shakēd suggested we ask our butcher if he could mince the fat for us, which was easy for him and made it even easier for us to render the fat.

Depending on the intended purpose of the tallow, you might want to remove as much meat as possible from the fat, which will result in a milder tallow.

You can render the fat in the oven, a slow cooker, a solar cooker, or on a cooktop. We often render fat in the winter inside a pot on top of the woodstove.

Rendering is best done on low heat to avoid burning any suspended particles, but hot enough to melt the fat. Mix the rendering fat several times to prevent burning at the bottom of the pot and to allow all the fat to render evenly. Depending on the size of the fat pieces, it could take you any time from an hour up to overnight cooking to completely render the fat. The rendering is complete when no more visible fat parts can be identified.

The next stage is to transfer the rendered fat into clean jars. We use large jars of 400 ml (14 fl oz) to 1 liter (35 fl oz) for storing tallow. Transferring the liquid is easy with a ladle, jam funnel, and sieve. You could use a larger sieve and transfer the liquid to another container, but it is best to minimize using a container that requires cleaning the fat. On top of the sieve, to reduce finer suspended particles, you could use a piece of cheesecloth. The cheesecloth will help create a clearer tallow and reduce the meat aromas. The cheesecloth can later be used as a great starter for a fire. We transfer the tallow while still hot to help create a seal.

Kūmara Fried in Tallow

Makes a large bowl of fries

Tallow is a versatile cooking fat, and is particularly suited for deep-frying. Fried kūmara, or sweet potato, is a favorite in our house. Tallow makes delicious fries—crispy on the outside and soft inside.

We love our fries with homemade mayo, Peanut Miso Vinegar Salad Dressing (see page 158), and, yes, ketchup.

1 liter (35 fl oz) tallow
1.5 kg (3 lb 5 oz) kūmara
Salt

Add the tallow to a deep frying pan or heavy-based pot and heat over a medium heat.

Prepare the kūmara for frying by washing and drying. We prefer to fry the kūmara unpeeled, but you can peel it if you like. Remove any undesired peel parts and cut the kūmara into relatively even sticks, about 1 cm (½ in) thick.

Once the tallow has heated to about 180–200°C (350–400°F), carefully add the kūmara sticks to the pan. With the quantity of tallow and kūmara in this recipe, you will need to divide the kūmara into three batches rather than attempt to fry them all at the same time. We find this makes better use of the tallow.

Every minute or so, stir the kūmara, so the frying is even. Once the kūmara has crisped to your liking, in about 7–12 minutes, carefully remove it from the pan with tongs or a skimmer, attempting to leave as much tallow behind as possible. We tend to use a wooden serving bowl, which can absorb some of the tallow, but you can use any bowl and line it with a paper towel. Salt to taste and serve while still warm.

Broth

Bone broth, also referred to as stock, is the liquid made from cooking animal bones.

We mostly make broth from beef, sheep, and chicken, but it can be made with fish, seafood, pork, and other poultry. A variety of herbs, vegetables, and spices can be used in addition to the bones to infuse extra taste and nutrition into the broth.

Broth can be made in any quantity, but with the bone size of ruminant animals it lends itself to be made in large quantities. When jarred hot, a seal is created and the broth will keep for up to 2 months in the fridge. Once opened, use the broth within 5 days. Broth can also be canned and stored in the pantry.

When we make broth, we usually season it with herbs and spices and sometimes add vinegar. While the research is contradictory, some research suggests that lowering the pH of the broth can moderately increase its mineral content.[*] Ultimately it is a matter of taste, so vinegar is optional.

Broth has been shown to have health benefits, including being anti-inflammatory,[†] and adding it to a dish is a great way to add flavor and texture. We use broth in our day-to-day cooking. We always have a jar ready for use in the fridge, and store various broths in the freezer. The quantity to add depends on the flavor profile of the broth, how much it is condensed, and the flavors in the dish we are making. If the dish is mild, we will use less broth so it doesn't dominate the dish; if we're using strong flavors, it is an opportunity to add more broth. We recommend starting with a smaller amount and increasing it gradually if you are serving it to people that aren't used to eating broth. If everyone relishes the broth addition, enjoy it lavishly, as there is little limit to the amount of broth you can consume.

We use it when cooking grains and legumes, and in stews, soups, stir-fries, mashed potatoes, or kūmara (sweet potatoes), sauces, glazes, fillings, breads, and bakes. Having broth at hand is also very useful when someone is unwell, as it can be diluted with water to make a simple soup, or better yet, served with miso.

Use fresh bought bones, or frozen or leftover from another dish, such as a roast. Use bones from free-range animals, and to help gel the broth, use bones that contain cartilage and marrow. Bones with meat will add a meaty flavor to the broth, while no meat will produce a milder flavor. You can also roast the bones in the oven before cooking them, which will add an additional flavor profile.

---

* H. N. Rosen, et al., "Chicken Soup Revisited: Calcium Content of Soup Increases with Duration of Cooking," *Calcified Tissue International* 54, no. 6 (June 1994): 486–88, https://doi.org/10.1007/BF00334329.

† Laura M. Mar-Solís, et al., "Analysis of the Anti-Inflammatory Capacity of Bone Broth in a Murine Model of Ulcerative Colitis," *Medicina* 57, no. 11 (20 October 2021): 1138, https://doi.org/10.3390/medicina57111138.

Bone Broth

Makes 4 liters (140 fl oz)

1–2 kg (2 lb 4 oz–4 lb 8 oz) bones of cows, sheep, pigs, poultry, or fish
Water
Salt
Vinegar (optional)
Herbs, spices and veggies of your choice (optional)

Place the bones in a heavy-based pot or slow cooker container that has the capacity to contain them with a few centimeters (couple of inches) above them. Occasionally we will have a bone that will poke out of the water, and we will turn it around several times during the cooking.

Cover the bones with water and bring to a slow boil without a lid. Once boiled, slightly reduce the heat even further. To produce a clearer broth, skim off the foam that develops at the surface at the beginning of the cooking process. After skimming, add some salt, some vinegar, if using, and, if desired, any other herbs, spices, or vegetables of your choice. Cover with a lid.

We suggest cooking the bone broth for at least 3 hours, but it can be cooked for longer. We often make bone broth when the woodstove is on, where it cooks overnight.

Depending on the types of bones used, bone broth will often have a fat layer, which, once cooled, can easily be removed. Let the pot's contents cool down and remove the floating solid fat. You can use this fat as you would use tallow (see page 316). Once removed, you can bring the broth back to a boil, cook it for 10 minutes, and then decant it into jars. Alternatively, you can skim as much fat off as you can while it is still hot.

Once thoroughly cooked and still hot, it is time to transfer the broth into clean jars. We use jars of 250 ml (9 fl oz) to 1 liter (35 fl oz), which gives us the flexibility of using a whole small jar in one dish, or opening a larger jar to be used throughout the week. Transferring the liquid is easy with a ladle, jam funnel, and sieve. You could use a larger sieve and transfer the liquid to another container. To create a clearer broth, line the sieve with cheesecloth to strain out the finer particles. The bottom 1 cm (½ in) of the pot will contain impurities that sank through cooking, so avoid pouring it into the jars. The bones can be added to the compost pile.

You can either process the jars through canning (see pages 258–63) or let them cool down to room temperature and store them in the fridge or freezer. If canning or storing in the freezer, leave enough headspace to allow the liquid to expand without breaking the jars.

Rice with Broth, Raisins & Cardamom

Serves 6

We had to stop ourselves from saying that every other recipe in the book is perfect on rice. But what can we say? We love rice, and we love topping it up with the goodness of our pantry. Rice served with eggs plus any ferment, pickle, miso, or preserve makes a fast, delicious lunch. A great way to increase the nutritional value of rice is to add broth instead of a portion of the cooking water.

The recipe below is a staple in our house. It's nutritious and aromatic, and the subtle taste of the broth is enjoyed by everyone.

2 cups white basmati rice
1 tablespoon fat from the broth, or tallow (see page 316), or olive oil
1 medium onion, diced or thinly sliced
10 g (¼ oz) salt
10 medium cardamom pods
¼ cup sesame seeds
¼ cup raisins
6 cloves garlic, chopped into thick pieces
½ cup broth
2 cups water

Rinse the rice until the water runs clear.

Place a pot over a medium heat and add the fat or oil, onion, and salt. Cook for 5 minutes, stirring regularly, until the onions start browning. Open the cardamom pods and add the cardamom seeds, sesame seeds, and raisins. Cook for 2–3 minutes, stirring well. Add the rice and stir. Add the garlic and stir thoroughly for 1 minute.

Pour the broth and cold water into the pot, mix well, and cover with a tight-fitting lid. Bring to a boil, then reduce to low heat and cook for 10 minutes. Do not stir or open the lid while cooking. Take off the heat and let the rice sit in the covered pot for 5 minutes before serving.

If not serving immediately, use a fork to fluff up the rice to release steam, and place the lid on the pot, leaving a small gap.

Final Words

Writing this book has been a huge undertaking, and more than we had ever anticipated, a deeply personal and emotional journey.

In *In Search of Lost Time*, Marcel Proust writes about the tremendous memory-evoking power tied to food, when eating a madeleine throws him back to his childhood. Many of the recipes in this book were equally evocative for us, the smells and the tastes like little capsules of times past. Some take us far back to our childhoods, the warmth of time spent with family, the strong hands of Grandma. The rituals of weekly gatherings. Memories of home.

Other recipes are tied strongly to our journey together, Niva and Yotam, learning about and experimenting with the wonderful world of ferments and preserves. Memories of our college dorms, our first flat where Yotam would bake us leftover grains bread every week, of our happy-go-lucky adventures in France and Italy, the time we spent in Costa Rica. Of lifelong friendships forged around the love of growing and preparing good food, and of our years here on Pākaraka Farm. Some recipes reached further into our personal and family histories, sometimes a thousand years back; the food itself a memory of lives long passed. There is so much of us in these pages, but when you make these recipes they will become yours.

We hope that when you do, you get to share them with loved ones, family and friends, that they lead you to adventures, new acquaintances, and happy memories, and make you feel at home.

Acknowledgments

We would like to extend our deepest appreciation to the incredible team at Allen & Unwin, who have been with us every step of the way. A huge thanks to publishing director Jenny who has shown unwavering support and trust in the direction, scope, and depth of this book. We are truly grateful for your guidance and belief in us.

To designer Megan and editor Síana, thank you so much for bringing and sharing your talent and working with us on this book. To project editor Kate, for doing everything to smooth things out through those final months, your efforts are greatly appreciated.

To photographer Aaron, a friend and fellow food-grower and thinker. We were so happy to be able to work with you on this book. Thank you for the care you took to understand what we wanted to convey and to help realise the images we had in our head with immense talent and skill so that we have the right and most beautiful photo for each recipe.

To food and prop stylist Jo, it was an absolute pleasure to get to know you and share your company during the photography session. We were stoked to have been working on this book with you and to benefit from your expertise to create not only stunning photographs but also those that reflect our culture and heritage.

To our family, we love you. Thank you to our daughters Lily and Dina. You are amazing—thank you for your patience and flexibility, your support and very honest feedback. You are the sunshine in our life. Blanche, Sara, Eitan, Dalia, Matty, Yuval, Naama, Teah, Aya, and Ella, thank you for your love. We couldn't have done this without you.

Special thanks to Yotam's grandma, Blanche, and aunt Keren—a huge thank you for supporting us in developing the Iraqi recipes in this book. To Niva's father, Eitan, and brother Yuval, a huge thank you for supporting us in developing the Yemeni recipes in this book. To Niva's mother, Sara, thank you for your huge help during the second photography session and for sending us beautiful tablecloths—family heirlooms that we are proud to have used in the book.

To Harry, our farm partner, for your love and support in everything we do and for creating an abundant farm.

To our dear friends Adi, Amanda, Anand, Dennis, Emma, Gaz, Ido, Jeremy, Juliette, Kerstie, Lou, Marie, Mea, Mike, Nancy, Sarah A., Sarah F., Shai, Shakēd, Simon, Tes, and so many others, thank you for being part of our fermentation journey, for sharing your experiences and for providing invaluable feedback on our endless streams of experiments.

We are incredibly grateful to Chika, our friend and miso teacher, who always made time to answer any questions we had while writing the koji chapter. To Eviatar, who serendipitously came to stay at the farm just as we were writing this book, and ended up not just helping in the garden but also baking with us, reviewing our sourdough recipes, and imparting his experience to help us make them that much better. To our dear friends Emma and Dennis for lending us their dehydrator at a crucial time when ours stopped working. To Sarah for giving us a new kombucha SCOBY, and sharing her experience of growing it in herbal teas. To Mea, Adi, Kerstie, and Amanda for wardrobe support. And finally, to Shakēd, who accepted any opportunity to make and test out family hand-down recipes and helped us keep our own grandmothers' recipes alive, we love feasting with you!

A huge thanks to our incredible gardening team here at Pākaraka, who helped us grow the beautiful vegetables you can see in the photos.

We thank those who have fermented and preserved foods over the millennia, as part of their lives, and those who will bear the fruits of the rich food cultures they inherit in years to come.

We also want to thank the vibrant communities of fermenters online from around the world, who continue to inspire us to dare to try new things and always find new ways to experiment. Your energy, passion, and willingness to share knowledge have been a constant source of inspiration for us, and for that, we are forever grateful.

Bibliography

Aayah, Hammoumi, Lahcen Ahansal, Jean-Pierre Guyot, Saad Ibnsouda, Isabelle Chevallier, and Abdellatif Boussaid. "Characterisation of the Dry Salted Process for the Production of the Msayer, a Traditional Lemon Aromatising Condiment." *LWT – Food Science and Technology* 43, no. 3 (April 2010): 568–72. https://doi.org/10.1016/j.lwt.2009.09.005.

Allahdo, Parviz, Javad Ghodraty, Heydar Zarghi, Zohre Saadatfar, Hassan Kermanshahi, and Mohammad Reza Edalatian Dovom. "Effect of Probiotic and Vinegar on Growth Performance, Meat Yields, Immune Responses, and Small Intestine Morphology of Broiler Chickens." *Italian Journal of Animal Science* 17, no. 3 (3 July 2018): 675–85. https://doi.org/10.1080/1828051X.2018.1424570.

Bonaterra, Gabriel A., Kevin Bronischewski, Pascal Hunold, Hans Schwarzbach, Ennio-U. Heinrich, Careen Fink, Heba Aziz-Kalbhenn, Jürgen Müller, and Ralf Kinscherf. "Anti-Inflammatory and Anti-Oxidative Effects of Phytohustil® and Root Extract of *Althaea officinalis* L. on Macrophages in Vitro." *Frontiers in Pharmacology* 11 (2020): 290. https://www.frontiersin.org/articles/10.3389/fphar.2020.00290.

Bortolomedi, Bruna Milena, Camila Souza Paglarini, and Fábio Cristiano Angonesi Brod. "Bioactive Compounds in Kombucha: A Review of Substrate Effect and Fermentation Conditions." *Food Chemistry* 385 (15 August 2022): 132719. https://doi.org/10.1016/ j.foodchem.2022.132719.

Budak, Nilgün H., Elif Aykin, Atif C. Seydim, Annel K. Greene, and Zeynep B. Guzel-Seydim. "Functional Properties of Vinegar." *Journal of Food Science* 79, no. 5 (May 2014): R757–64, https://doi.org/10.1111/1750-3841.12434.

Castellone, Vincenzo, Elena Bancalari, Josep Rubert, Monica Gatti, Erasmo Neviani, and Benedetta Bottari. "Eating Fermented: Health Benefits of LAB-Fermented Foods." *Foods* 10, no. 11 (31 October 2021): 2639. https://doi.org/10.3390/foods10112639.

Chattopadhyay, R. R., S. K. Bhattacharyya, S. K. Bhattacharyya, and S. K. Bhattacharyya. "Herbal Spices as Alternative Antimicrobial Food Preservatives: An Update." *Pharmacognosy Reviews* 1, no. 2 (2007): 239–47.

Chitrakar, Bimal, Min Zhang, and Benu Adhikari. "Dehydrated Foods: Are They Microbiologically Safe?" *Critical Reviews in Food Science and Nutrition* 59, no. 17 (2019): 2734–45. https://doi.org/10.1080/10408398.2018.1466265.

Doner, Landis W. "The Sugars of Honey—A Review." *Journal of the Science of Food and Agriculture* 28, no. 5 (May 1977): 443–56. https://doi.org/10.1002/jsfa.2740280508.

Feizollahi, Ehsan, Razieh Sadat Mirmahdi, Alaleh Zoghi, Ruurd T. Zijlstra, M. S. Roopesh, and Thava Vasanthan. "Review of the Beneficial and Anti-Nutritional Qualities of Phytic Acid, and Procedures for Removing It from Food Products." *Food Research International (Ottawa, Ont.)* 143 (May 2021): 110284. https://doi.org/10.1016/j.foodres.2021.110284.

Frakolaki, Georgia, Virginia Giannou, Evangelos Topakas, and Constantina Tzia. "Chemical Characterization and Breadmaking Potential of Spelt versus Wheat Flour." *Journal of Cereal Science* 79 (1 January 2018): 50–56. https://doi.org/10.1016/j.jcs.2017.08.023.

García-Burgos, María, Jorge Moreno-Fernández, María J.M. Alférez, Javier Díaz-Castro, and Inmaculada López-Aliaga. "New Perspectives in Fermented Dairy Products and Their Health Relevance." *Journal of Functional Foods* 72 (September 2020): 104059. https://doi.org/10.1016/j.jff.2020.104059.

Index